CHANGE MAKERS
Four Stories

of

Ordinary people demonstrating the art of combining people-power, media coverage, and working with political leaders to accomplish lasting change.

By

Carla Brooks Johnston

ISBN: 0984248935
ISBN-13: 9780984248933

Published by

PARLANCE

P.O. 391114
Cambridge, MA 02139

To
Ordinary people who become extraordinary people because they take initiative, show courage and persistence in being change makers

To
Lester Ralph who stayed Mayor long enough for the systemic changes to take root creating a legacy that still lasts 40+ years later.

To
The scores of Somerville heroes named and unnamed in the First Story. You each still make lives better because of your contribution to that remarkable time that we all spent together as change makers.

To
Josephine Murray, George Sommaripa, Clifford Truesdell, Matthew Leighton, Peter Dyke, Marilyn Braun, Peter Koff, Pam Kelly, Newell Mack and hundreds of courageous First Responders who wanted to be sure that government was honest when it said it would protect the American population.

To
Fred Salvucci, Bob Kiley, Michael Dukakis, Dick Wall, Fran Meany, George McCarthy, Eleanor Shea, Linda Marcellino, Sue Tamber and scores of public officials and MBTA civil servants who dared to find and implement service improvements and cost cuts.

To
The Elected Officials of the Lee County Florida 2007 MPO who had the courage to ask Congress to fix the tampered earmark from Alaska. To Darla Letourneau whose research and networking skills kept the focus on fixing this earmark in Congress. To Senator Nelson, and Congressman Mack and their staffs, especially Stacy Smith and Jeff Cohen, to Keith Ashdowne and those in the media who covered this story until Congress voted.

And To
Robert L. Hilliard, my companion for over a quarter century. He insists that manuscripts can be finished, and he's a change maker. As a Private in WWII, he and an army buddy wrote the letters that eventually reached President Truman who investigated and ordered General Eisenhower to improve Holocaust survivors treatment. (NYT 9/30/45)

Carla Brooks Johnston 1940 - 2011

Up to her last days Carla Johnston worked on editing proofs of this book, leaving it as a legacy of how to make our communities and the world a better place. She hoped that the true stories in this book would encourage readers to become change makers, to join the ordinary people in this book who became extraordinary by getting involved in solving the problems of the worlds in which they lived.

Carla believed that each of us can be a change maker, simply by talking with friends, engaging with our communities, working with the media and working with those that have the power to make things happen--our elected officials. Each of us can bring about meaningful, sustainable and lasting changes to improve our communities and the world.

All income from this book and tax deductible contributions from readers and the public, will go to New Century Policies Educational Programs, Inc. (NCPEP) a non-profit organization which Carla founded in 1982. The intent is to launch a seed funding grant program for Change Makers--individuals and community organizations that are prepared to make positive and sustainable changes that will benefit their communities.

New Century Policies Educational Programs, Inc.,
P.O. Box 113,
Sanibel, FL 33957
http://www.CarlaBrooksJohnston.com

Also by Carla Brooks Johnston

- Raising Myself: A Teenager's Odyssey, Cambridge, MA: Parlance, 2010. Available on www.amazon.com
- Screened Out: How theMedia Control Us and What We Can Do About It, Armonk, N.Y.: M.E. Sharpe, 2000.
- Global News Access: Impact of New Communications Technologies, Westport, CT & London: Praeger, 1998.
- Winning the Global TV News Game, Boston and London: Butterworth-Heinemann/Focal & Broadcasting & Cable, 1995. (The '90s revolution in global access to news)
- "China to Korea by Ferry," The New York Times, New York, June 6, 1993.
- "The Press and The Electoral Process," The Radcliffe Quarterly, Cambridge, MA: Radcliffe College, Vol. 78 No. 2, June 1992. (Visit to Moscow: Observer at Russia's first Presidential election in 1991.)
- International Television Co-Production, Boston and London: Butterworth-Heinemann/Focal Press, 1992
- Election Coverage: Blueprint for Broadcasters, Boston and London: Butterworth-Heinemann/Focal Press, 1991.
- Local Initiatives for Affordable Housing, Boston: New Century Policies, 1989. (Local government's options)
- Reversing the Nuclear Arms Race. Cambridge, MA: Schenkman Books, 1986. Forward by Gene R. LaRocque, Rear Admiral USN (Ret.) (Influences on policy making)
- Under the Interstate. Boston, MA: MA Department of Community Affairs and the National Endowment for the Arts, 1975. Editor. Winner of NEA Nationwide City Options Competition. Focus: Ethnic Heritage in Immigrant City.

Table of Contents

Counterpoint One

Skeptics on Value or Liklihood of Making Public Policy Change

"I elect someone to public office and I expect that they will turn things around—give him or her six months, max," the man in the turtleneck sweater said as he exited the club car.

"You're absolutely right," said the woman finishing her scotch-and-soda and preparing to leave. "I got all excited about this new movement to streamline government. Cut the fat. Cut the sloppiness. Run it like a corporation. We're over-taxed. We had a lot of victories in the election. But now they'd better deliver. I look for the headline everyday." She slammed the club car door behind her.

The people who just left this AMTRAC club car were talking about whether or not public policy change is practically possible. They were in animated conversation about macro-economics, globalization and edicts from top national leadership. They've left now, leaving five of us still talking. It's just us—Richard, John, Paul, Ted and me, Carla.

"You'd think you could change national policy or culture or politics or anything in a single 30-second command—the way you hold a bone and tell the dog to 'sit.'" Richard's dog analogy is where we begin our stories and the counterpoint.

The five of us settle into seats at one end of the club car, close enough to hear each other and far enough to keep our own space.

I start. "Change making has always been of interest to me. I think it's worth looking at what's behind the language we use. Maybe it's just because I've wandered through all these fields in the decades of my career that I am tempted to see if there's a common meaning behind the language. In a bus station, a change-maker breaks your money into the types of coins that you need in order to accomplish your objective of getting where you want to go. In a business setting or political setting, a change-maker is one who promises (or who actually does) change policy or paradigm from the current policy that is deemed less than satisfactory to something new, and you have hope that the new policy will be more satisfactory—whatever satisfactory may mean for you, your wallet, or those you care about. In the Bible, the money changer was the guy thrown out of the temple for distracting people from important matters because he diverted attention toward ordinary life. Yet in the story, Jesus holds a coin and reminds the audience that we all live in both worlds, inseparable. In a casino, the change-maker turns your currency into the currency needed to play their games—the ones one hopes to win."

"Had you noticed," I continued, "that change making has similar characteristics regardless of the situation. The process of making change is always inspired by hope for something better, but is never without detailed transactions. Change making is never an activity for people who are happy with the status quo. Over the centuries and from venue to venue a great many people hold hope that things can be better, even though they never know exactly what will be the results of change. They remain eager to give up something that they have for hope."

"So?" John, the most outspoken of us, says. "I still think that all you get out of this rhetoric about change making is a bunch of people protesting, picketing, or a group of 1970s women burning their bras, or a suicide bomber—some dramatic, irrational act that just gives sane people a headache. All it amounts to is a 90-second blip on the evening news."

I respond. "You've certainly picked up on a common stereotype about change making--just a bunch of 'troublemakers', people complaining. Yes, surely there are times when single individuals, or groups of people, or these days thousands of text messages from cell phones seek to 'make a point.' Sometimes those single incidents are not a basis for constructive change, but simply intended to vent someone's anger or 'spring fever'. Sometimes these events raise very important issues that should not be dismissed, but are dismissed because the tactics are too offensive to those who should hear. Sometimes, single high-profile and emotional pleas for change making are a deliberate part of a more substantive effort to make new policy—a single strategic move as part of something that will win enough popular support to become an unstoppable change. It's been said that whenever 25% of the population in the United States, favors a particular change, it becomes nearly impossible for some form of it not to actually be implemented.[1]"

"Making change never happens in one dramatic act" I say. "It's silly that people get all excited one minute. 'Expect change with the next election,' they scream. Then a few months after the election, when the change--however you define that--hasn't yet happened, the same people change their tune. 'See, they failed.' Then they say, 'Throw them out; we need new people.' This only sets a masochistic framework for constant disappointment destined to pull us all into the problem, not the solution. It fails to think through all the steps needed to explain new policy to stakeholders, the legal steps required in a country of law, not personal whim, and the steps needed to select key people and enable them to actually implement the desired change. You'd think people would think it through. After all, any average person knows it takes more than a single dramatic act to rearrange their home furniture, or to switch jobs. Because we believe 'twitters' and 'sound-bites' tell us the truth, do we now also believe in instant gratification?"

"In my opinion," I continue, "making change in public policy requires a lot of what might be called 'nickel and diming'—linking major strategy to small tactical steps involving countless individuals, most of them just typical individuals."

"You can't change nothing,' you know that! Besides, why would you want to?" That was John. John sat at a table across the aisle. He was 60ish, loose tie, wrinkled suit. Obviously, he wasn't pleased to be riding for so long on a train, not a plane, and with us who were not his usual set of friends.

"Besides," he says, looking at me, "what's a girl got to say about anything?"

John thought he knew all the answers. After all, at this point in his career, he should, right? From what he's said earlier, we knew that he wheeled-and-dealed in real estate development—always ready to make a deal that benefited him more than any of the other stakeholders. He always won, so he indicated. His circle of colleagues included people who mattered. By choice or by circumstance they were all men of similar background. No point listening to others. From John's perspective, it didn't matter whether or not others had other views, he had power. He and his friends *were* power representing business, local government and the bankers. Wasn't that the same as truth?

John says, "I don't know why you waste time thinking about change making. As long as we have law and order and the status quo stays put, all is just fine. Best country on earth, it is!"

Clatter, clatter. Lights flicker. The rail is not always smooth. It's the middle of the night. Most folks have gone to bed. The weather and the airline cancellations brought us all together on this train. It's the fastest way, the only option remaining, to get where we need to go.

"Well, maybe she has a point when she says that things can change," said Paul.

Paul, in his late 50s, a baby-boomer, his red baseball cap pulled low over his forehead, was sprawled across the two seats just behind me, using his carry-on bag for a pillow.

"Things can change, Paul continued. "Once in a while they get better than they used to be. For example, once in a while, I get a better car, or the street by my house is repaved, or they build a new movie theater or a new ball field. Once in a while, my stock portfolio even gets better. All I have to do was wait and watch—and pay. I don't really like the paying part—especially paying taxes. They gotta be ripping me off. Somebody ought to do something about that," Paul concluded and hit the table with his fist.

Paul didn't take much too seriously. His world included only him. 'Big picture' things were peripheral. Paul just liked to play. He could afford to, so why not? Besides, who would know where to begin to make change? Paul knew it would take time away from what he cared about to figure out how to go about changing anything and, even then, succeeding was a long shot. Life is short. Why not play if you can do it?

Richard was sitting across the aisle from John, also at a club car table. He was in his mid-forties. His feet were up on the opposite bench and he'd taken his shoes off. He'd been reading a magazine. He looked like he might be a professor or maybe a doctor. He looked up from behind his glasses.

"If you really look into what kind of a world we're leaving to our kids, can you be proud? If you shrug off thinking about this by saying, 'I'm in charge, that's enough' or 'all I can do is watch anyway,' can you live with yourself? I want my kids to know that I tried to do something with my life. I try to make the changes that improve their quality of life. I want to die knowing that my life mattered. That's about more than making money or making a bet on a game."

Richard ducked back into the pages of his magazine saying, "I may not change much, but I have to say that I tried. Otherwise, I'm wasting my life, aren't I?

Ted joined the conversation. Ted had already passed his business card to the rest of us from his nearby seat. He was Vice-President of Media Incorporated. He was clearly on the fast track for success—to make lots of money with all the bells and whistles that command public acknowledgment.

"Look, the world is divided into investors and consumers," Ted said. Who cares what way people swing, or why, in elections? If we're going to make money, we need them to swing one way today, then the other way next year. Otherwise, the public will lose interest and candidates will stop spending on media. Who cares if 'change' happens, whatever change means? It's like Darwin said. You either survive or you don't. If my company survives, that's all that matters. Why would I think about the consequences of not surviving? That's what happens in those wretched poverty-infested countries where people don't even have the incentive to go earn a living."

I re-enter this conversation. Maybe because I'm the only woman in the club car, I sit at my own table. I like that distance from the others.

"I think you're painting this canvas with a pretty broad brush," I say. "You're leaving out a lot of details that, if not tended to, could matter even to you. I know you'd probably prefer seeing an x-rated movie over hearing what I'm saying about change making, but I'd like to tell you a few stories of just plain ordinary people who did make change that mattered to hundreds of thousands of people, they might even matter to you."

"Change making," I continue, "is a dimension that can be added to anyone's life regardless of profession or situation. I became interested because I grew up on my own[2] and consequently was a sort of spectator in the world around me, watching what 'normal people' did. I had cousins in Rochester who lived the way you--John and Paul and Ted--do. Their lives seemed pretty boring to me. I watched and heard about fascinating things that all sorts of other people were engaged in, problems people were trying to solve. This other world seemed so much bigger than the world in which my cousins lived. It would offer real challenge and it could matter, not in terms of dollars, but in terms of interest and real value. As years went on and I completed my university studies, I decided that those whose lives mattered most were those who spent energy, skill and hard work trying to improve the quality of life for those around them. Sedentary comfort at the top of the success ladder—labeled by power, wealth, prestige seemed to lack the challenge I wanted. I looked more at how power, wealth and prestige might be used to upgrade value for the larger body of people—create new opportunities. I was impressed by the persons throughout history who have accomplished that as actual change-makers—in the 20th century people like

Mahatma Gandhi and Martin Luther King Jr. and Dietrich Bonhoeffer. Besides, I figured life is too short to waste on being bored. If change making is hoping for something better, and working for something better, I'm all in favor of that. Always a challenge. Always an adventure. Over the generations people have improved the status quo. Why not? So I care about change-makers."

"I don't think great sudden things happen to improve lives," I continued. "As Richard said a few minutes ago, making change is not like commanding the dog to 'sit'. Most change comes in nickels and dimes—the efforts of one individual and then another and another to take actions that can result in something that improves one's conditions. It's amazing to watch. Those who decide to not simply complain or opt out, but to help create change, do change. They themselves find new resolve, new energy, new joy in the midst of the nasty job of challenging things that need to be challenged. I've got four stories to tell you. Each is very different from the other. The first involves huge citizen efforts, lots of media and political activity. The others focus on different ways to make change with different kinds of media involvement, different reasons for elected and appointed officials to make 'change' to benefit their self-interest, and far less involvement from the public. After I tell you the stories, I'd like to hear your reactions. "

"O.K." says Paul. "I got nothing better to do on this slow train ride. Besides, maybe I'll hear if anyone's figured out how to get government to tax us less."

John just shrugs his shoulders.

"Go ahead," says Richard.

"Might as well," says Ted, "It'll pass the time. Maybe I'll get some new angles for future media programming. On the other hand, we, like other media, are really into entertainment. Public affairs only matters when there's a revolution or something dramatic enough to get the public's attention."

The First Story: Somerville, Massachusetts— Decaying City

Ordinary People Turn Their City Around

INDIVIDUALS, CIVIC GROUPS, AN ELECTION, A NEW MAYOR, AND MAJOR MEDIA

"It's Somerville, Massachusetts, February 18, 1971. This aging industrial city of nearly 90,000 people jammed into less than four square miles, it is standing room only in the High School Auditorium. Multiple generations of blue-collar and poor families, people with a lot of heart and integrity, hadn't had access to much privilege and had had it with their local government. About four years earlier, a few individuals decided that they were tired of being charged too much, served too poorly, and taken for granted by arrogant politicians. I can tell you this story because I was there. It's not my story. I simply was witness to incredible acts of thousands of individuals and of the overwhelming impact they had on the spirit and the resulting change they made for thousands of persons in their city. I'll never forget this story. Here it is." I comment to my fellow passengers in the club car.

"Tar him. Feather him."[1] The public shouts at the City Auditor on the High School Auditorium stage.

The mayor is interrupted dozens of times during his speech with long cheers, applause and foot-stamping, as well as cat-calls, boos, and shouts of 'ride them out' and 'get rid of them all' when he mentions the politicians whose actions were detailed in the stories," reported on the front page of the *Boston Globe* every day that week. [2]

"We came to save the city from crooks." One person shouts.

"So are you a registered voter?" someone shouted at her.

"No, but I will be in the morning."[3] She replies. "I didn't care. But now I know why I should."

A reformer had been elected Mayor—an Episcopal priest who was also a lawyer, a young man thrown into this sea of snakes with little preparation. This meeting of the Board of Aldermen is called in order to have the new Mayor explain to the public what the *Boston Globe* had had as headlines everyday that week—how corruption had picked the pockets of unsuspecting taxpayers. The City Auditor tries to deny any implication of graft, but he is shouted down by the standing room only angry audience. Much to the relief of the police, the fire marshal, and those of us with jobs in the new city administration, the meeting is declared adjourned--quickly, before things got out of hand. That mob *really* could have lynched him.

"It's the first time I really understood the mob psychology that led to the lynchings of a half century earlier in the southern United States. It's unbelievable. Comes to no good end for anyone," I told my fellow passengers in the club car who are listening. "Thankfully, the crowd dispersed peacefully."

Jim Bretta, a local priest was one of three of us who served as executive staff in the new mayor's office recalled the meeting: "It was frightening. It was one of the scariest experiences of my life. I remember the fever pitch. I remember feeling the anger of people that night. Part of it is that nobody likes to think that he or she has been deceived personally. But beyond that, to have your whole community put in a state wide position of such disrepute on the front page of the main newspaper in the state, every day for a week, you feel that not only have you personally been deceived, personally injured. It's a pall on the whole community." [4]

How did a group of 60's idealists who believed that individuals could make a difference in advancing human rights, good schools, honest corporations, and responsible government ever get to this point? We believed in orderly government; we weren't radicals. We hated violence. A number of us, whose idealism transcended our different backgrounds and experiences, had been meeting and began to work together to make life better for typical families, to get our tax dollars worth. The pols didn't like it! We didn't give up! We learned how to win! We did win! In 1969, we won City Hall, fought the battle to win lasting local government reform, and learned how to create and sustain policy innovation. Amazingly, a lot was accomplished, and now—a half century later—these accomplishments serve today's generation.

In 1971, the *Boston Globe* won a Pulitzer Prize for this investigative reporting of corruption in Somerville. In 1973, the National Municipal Association granted the coveted *All American Cities Award* to Somerville because citizens worked constructively with government to end the patterns of decay and to build a city vital with programs, new infrastructure and, most important, with a new ethic for doing business.

To my train companions I say, "See, it is ordinary citizens who turn an ineffectual, allegedly corrupt city 360 degrees— and sustain the change. Together, these individuals really "make change." I tell them how they did it.

Somerville is a place everyone was abandoning. Flight to the suburbs result in population decline from the 1940s high of 105,000 to 88,000 by 1970. But Somerville is still one of the nation's most densely populated cities. The *Boston Globe* described it as "one of Boston's oldest bedroom communities (which) faces many of her big sister's problems with far less money to solve them. The atmosphere was one of decay: narrow, pot-holed streets; rows of two and three family houses; dingy store fronts lining the main street and shivering senior citizens clustered at bus stops." [5] This is the same place where rebel British immigrants raised the first American flag on January 1, 1776. In the 1970s, the city is still mostly immigrants-- but from other backgrounds. They are Irish, Greek, Italians, French Canadians, Portuguese, Jews, Haitians, some Asians and African Americans. An American Bi-centennial oral history paints the picture of the '70s in Somerville; here are some of the comments made by immigrants:

- "I was born and brought up here in Brickbottom, right on the spot where the incinerator stands today. In my house we always spoke Greek; not a word of English was heard. Outside it was the same. All the grocers and all the general stores were owned by Greeks."

- "My Italian grandfather taught me responsibility. He used to go out and shovel the walks so that people could go to church. Now, nobody cares."

- "All my family is here now which makes us very happy. You cannot explain the difference unless you have lived in Portugal to a certain age and realize how bad the system was. Over here, it's completely different government wise, and you're finally free to be able to pick up the newspaper and read about the government inside and outside the US."

- "The housing may not be great by American standards, but it's a hundred times better than housing in Haiti."

- I owned a lot of real estate in Shanghai. I lost it all when the communists took over--lost everything. My wife and I came here. Eventually we bought a house in Somerville. There are other Chinese people nearby. My children are all educated. One has a Ph.D., another is a doctor. It's hard here now. I'm alone. I don't know how to cook. I don't want to bother the children."

- "Many veterans in the city belong to two or three posts. Those who are entitled to belong to the Disabled Veteran Post like to be at that one. Those who are entitled to honor because they served overseas like to join the VFW. Most of us join posts for sociability." [6]

- "There were a number of Jewish families living near the synagogue here. It was OK until I began to go to elementary school in the 1930s. In the boy's bathroom, they'd tease us because we were circumcised. At Christmas and Easter they'd chase us and call us Christ killers." [7]

The mosaic of Somerville is more complex than its physical characteristics or the cultural viewpoints of its people. Well before the 1970s, major national economic shifts created challenged to old cities. Those who were economically successful bought their first cars and helped to create the new affluent suburbs. Economic segregation, not much of an issue pre-World War II, would be more of a societal challenge than racial segregation. In this climate, those who want change walked into City Hall in 1970 to run the city—a group of young idealists who had never ever run a multi-million dollar corporation. The money is gone. Across the country only 10% of the population controls 70% of the nation's wealth, and that 10% has no interest in Somerville.

"We aren't about changing the economic system or the distribution of wealth. That is too ideological for us, and seemingly pointless. We are about more achievable objectives, encouraging individuals to understand that if the quality of life is to be better for their children and if they are to be less exploited, they alone need to put into practice the kind of life they hope for—one that respects the value of everyone's hopes, one where each person can learn how to end the hostility and anger and to begin the future."

The *Boston Globe's* "Spotlight Series," states that "the problems facing Somerville--insufficient tax base, politically inspired inefficiency, taxpayers impatience--are hitting more and more towns every day. Their solution depends on leadership and dedication--both of which may have found their way into Somerville today." [8]

It had taken just five years--from 1965 to 1970--for the citizens to take charge of their lives and redirect their municipal government to reflect their concerns.

ASSEMBLING THE TEAM--THE EARLY DAYS

Before 1965, there were no 'letters to the editor' in the local paper. There was no 'talk radio' addressing local civic issues. Civic advocacy groups didn't exist--only 'service clubs' mostly for the local businessmen and clergymen. There weren't even active PTA's. The men worked hard, mostly in blue collar jobs; the women struggled with limited budget and limited opportunity to do their best for large families. People bristled at the arrogance and questionable competence of government; but the prevailing belief was that 'you can't fight city hall.' People had dreams for their kids and for their community but, trapped in the unending routine of work, it was hard to see that things could be any different from the day-to-day routine. There were no pre-school programs, or teen centers, or elderly programs. No neighborhood health clinics existed, no community policing. Schools were deteriorating. Public housing was deteriorating. Even the fire houses and police station were deteriorating from neglect.

But the city was plastered with political signs during election season—as if one day's election could really bring and sustain a better life—just one day's vote by itself. Bob Hilliard, a local teacher who later became the campaign manager for our 1970's reform mayor, remembers how, as a kid, he pitched in at election time. "To be brought up in Somerville in the 1950s and 1960s was to be politically active. I remember passing out stickers for Andy Capuano, the mayoral candidate in 1953 (father of the future U.S. Congressman). I was only 10. We were neighborhood kids. After we played baseball, we'd give the candidate a hand." [9]

Somerville's political activity wasn't just local. Former Speaker of the U.S. House of Representatives, Thomas P. "Tip" O'Neill (who happened to be my neighbor), represents Somerville in Washington. He was first elected in 1952, barely beating Michael LoPresti, the popular Italian from Boston's South End. So, during the early 1960's when another popular Italian, the new Somerville Mayor Larry Bretta (uncle of the reform administration's Jim Bretta), rose to power in the Eighth Congressional District there was increasing talk of his 'taking on the Congressman.' To avoid this risk, Tip arranged an offer that Bretta couldn't refuse--a lucrative and prominent appointment in the General Services Administration in Washington. His unfinished mayoral term was completed by the pleasant, but not imaginative Jim Brennan, who had the misfortune to serve just as Somerville's own 1960's civic reform movement reached maturity.

Bob Hilliard summarized why the reform movement arose: "Somerville had had an unusually bad wave of people with no vision. I think most of them thought they were doing something for their community, but mostly, they were in it for the rewards that could be gotten for being a public servant in those days." [10]

The political flurry and prominence of elected officials had not really changed life for the typical citizen. For most people, "self-government" was a text book term disconnected from the real world. People weren't welcome in City Hall. And, most people were too tired, too uninformed, or too busy to consider the implications of governing themselves.

I add, "Typical citizens then, as now a half century later, don't need political pundits to tell them something is wrong.

Then, as now, they are angry and frustrated and uncertain about how to fix things. Somerville Housing Project tenant and widow, Winnie Lawrence, had spent her life in Somerville. Without income or job experience, she relied on welfare to pay her family's bills.

Winnie described the city in 1965, "We must have all went to sleep to let people come in and tear down our community." [11]

But timing *is* everything. The seeds of reform in Somerville of the 1960s and 1970s are sown by the wind sweeping across the entire United States--the John F. Kennedy presidency, the Lyndon Johnson war on poverty, Martin Luther King Jr.'s dream for civil rights, and the anger of citizens that finally put an end to the inexplicable war in Vietnam. Somerville's emerging reformers are caught in the national social environment of the era. Belief in our ability to succeed fuels our activity locally, as it does what's happening nationally.

Somerville housewife and activist leader Pat LaColla explains her beliefs. "Don't forget," she says, "Jack Kennedy said 'Don't ask what your country can do for you; ask what you can do for your country.' That's what it is about. We believed that we could change the world. He led you to believe that." [12] This belief would lead Pat and her husband Nick, a truck driver for Table Talk Pies, to move mountains for the kids of Somerville helping to coalesce the citywide reform movement.

Maureen Amerol Hilliard, (Bob's wife) began her elementary school teaching career during the growth of the school reform movement that began our journey into politics. Later she became the city Election Commissioner. Maureen, who had grown up in Somerville comments on why she got involved:

"Youth are invigorated by Kennedy. We are the children of the post-war era. Women are becoming more powerful and we thought we could have a voice. My mother couldn't even teach after she got married. I was a teacher. The 1960s was a different time." [13]

Other venues brought people into what became a city-wide "we can fix what's broken" movement. Quite by accident, the concern for civil rights that brings some of us together in Somerville would lead us far beyond our initial intentions.

In 1965, my college friend and Methodist minister George Hover and people from Crane Theological Seminary at Tufts University created the fledgling Somerville Racial Understanding Committee (SRUC)—the first of the fledgling citywide grassroots civic groups. How could anyone ignore civil rights given the national prominence of Dr. Martin Luther King Jr.'s non-violent campaign? Somerville is about 95% white, but the small black population is a well-educated community that established roots here to 'escape the ghetto of Roxbury.' They settled in Somerville early in the 20th century.

"SRUC is a mixture of people," remembers Pearl Morrison, then a young parent from the city's African American neighborhood and later to become the first black elementary school principal. "A number of the whites in SRUC were people who had recently moved into the city, but also people whose roots were here. What made that so wonderful is that those of us who had our roots here always knew that we needed an organization like this, but we weren't sure we could assume the initiative to make it happen. The people who came from the 'outside' so to speak, for some reason, are able to do this. I think it is because they are not known. So no one paid attention to the organization when it started. I think the mentality among the city fathers is that 'these people are in someone's living room jawboning about what's going on, but they won't raise much dust. So let them be. You and I really know that they don't have the power. We have the power. [14]

"My mother, Annie Johnson," Pearl says, "got me involved in SRUC. I was restless because I had just gotten my masters degree and I wasn't allowed to teach because I was pregnant. I had all this energy that was not being tapped. My mother had grown up in Somerville and in 1943 bought the house where we grew up. It was a mixed neighborhood–Italian, Greek, African American and Irish. It was a great place to grow up. We weren't intimidated by the majority race because we grew up together. Those of us who are black could traverse any economy, any culture, and any group. We know how to interface, how to relate."

Pearl continues, "I think my mother became an activist because she so often heard her grandmother, my great-grandmother, tell about the old south–Lexington, Kentucky. My great-grandmother lived through the Civil War. She passed on all these stories. Because my mother was an only child, she was always with older people. She heard lots of stories of injustice, but she was always told you have to be prepared. You have to get an education. You know the stories about the 'house-negro' and the 'field-negro.' My great-grandmother would always tell my mother, you know you're not a 'field-negro.' We are 'house-negroes.' We are all able to read. So, all of my mothers family is very well educated and well spoken. She believes that, at any time, her kids can find themselves living under the onus of injustice and have to know how to deal with it. Hearing about the lynching of my great-grandmother's brother, no doubt, strengthened my mother's resolve to be active and be prepared." [15]

Pearl summarizes, "I chaired SRUC for two years. Everything we do had never been done before in Somerville. Consequently, everything we do, not only affects civil rights, but affects the overall civic climate—creating a climate for change, and inspiring us to make change. We run workshops for teachers at Tufts on *multi-culturalism*—a foreign concept in the 1960s. We take a diverse group of kids to the United Nations in New York City—the first time many had left Somerville. We broker fair housing altercations. In 1966, we begin a pilot program with the Experiment in International Living's cross-cultural exchange. Only, our cross-cultural exchange is within the USA. We bring black students from Tupelo, Mississippi to live as family members with white families for the summer while they get better paying jobs than could be found in Mississippi. We create a summer multi-racial day camp thanks to donated space from the First Baptist Church. We arrange for the school libraries to acquire multi-racial books. When school principals, like the one at the Lowe School, refuses to follow through, parents raise the money to buy the books and made a public donation to the school—complete with newspaper photographer. As result of the publicity, Sears Roebuck gives the school an award for its civil rights initiatives. The principal, of course, is pleased to receive the award. And we, as local activists, begin our education on how to deal successfully with intransigent bureaucrats so that change can be sustained.

"Finally, in 1970, when Mayor Ralph is elected," Pearl Morrison says, "my mother went to discuss the participation of people from Somerville's black community in the Fourth of July Parade. You see, the kids keep asking my mother–how come they don't let blacks march in the parade? She got the St. Richards marching band from a school in Roxbury to agree to come, and she got Mayor Ralph to agree to let them march and in 1970 we saw our first black marching band."

"You see," I say to my train car companions as I continue with this story, "making change is easy. It's one person deciding to meet with the Mayor with a hard to refuse suggestion. It's not complaining. It's a small thing, a simple thing. Change happens in nickel and dime decisions that have an impact on thousands of people over the decades. All that is required is for this individual to have an idea and commit to the initiative and detailed steps required to make it turn into reality. She keeps up the spirit to persist and to involve others until a problem is solved. Bite off the small stuff—not huge intangibles."

I tell the club car passengers more about Pearl Morrison who says: "Before 1970, you saw one black in business circles, two in the teaching ranks. There was a big athlete. But no blacks worked in the stores near out neighborhood. There were no blacks in public works, no black policeman, no black fireman, no black veterans post members, and no black elected officials."[16] SRUC activities suggests alternatives, and, because we are relatively low profile and non-threatening, we have the freedom to assemble the people and the programs that result in a more inclusive community. Small things change, quietly become a new norm, and steps toward racial integration just became O.K. Surely, there were many painful incidents, but with persistence opportunities improve and we know we're moving forward."

"Each of these separate activities brought in new persons," I tell those in the club car. My neighbor, Harvard graduate student Maris Vinovskis, wrote a letter to the SRUC post office box expressing an interest in civil rights and politics. He not only becomes active in SRUC, but later he becomes treasurer for Lester Ralph's campaign for Mayor.

BUILDING A CITY-WIDE CIVIC MOVEMENT

As we branched out from these early involvements into seeking city-wide civic improvements, the focus was kids and the quality of education offered to them. The track record hadn't been good. Some forty percent dropped out of high school. People in East Somerville begin their own civic activism. In East Somerville, a street based organization, The Franklin Avenue Neighborhood Group (FANG), starts.

Gloria Albano tells how she and her husband, Sal, later to become a state senator, start it. "In the early 1960s Sal and I came back from Germany with a cookoo clock and a baby. My husband was drafted out of college (Boston University) and in January '59 he was sent to Germany. In Germany when we ran a teen club, our first encounter with civic organizations. When we came back to the States, my mother-in-law was ill. She owned a two-family house on Franklin Avenue. It was in total disarray. She asked us to move to the second floor and she would live on the first floor. So we did it.

"At the time, I was living in Arlington," Gloria Albano continues, "an older suburb a few miles further out from Boston.

25

East Somerville is like a foreign country to me. It is so *city*. You have H.P. Hood, Schrafft Chocolates, more industry and tons of people in a very small area. Franklin Avenue needs a lot of help. That end of the city has been deteriorating for years. Wonderful people live there, people who have lived there all their lives, raised their children, and the children had their children. We need off street parking so the fire trucks can get through. We have the old cobblestone streets and we need the streets paved. There are junk cars, just dropped, some fire-bombed. People just don't know what to do. People don't know then that if you get a whole bunch of people and you register them to vote, City Hall will listen. We don't know that then. That was the beginning of knowing that the power *is* the people, just as much as money is. It's always been in my nature to problem solve, even now. So we start talking to the neighbors. It isn't hard because Sal had grown up with these people.

"We are young," Gloria said. "We trust people and we think we can make a difference. We want the quality of our lives and for our children's lives to be better. My husband has such pride in his neighborhood. He wants to make it better not only for himself and his family but for everybody else's family. The city government is talking about "urban renewal"—basically 'urban removal'—getting us all out so they can put more commercial development in. Everybody comes to my house one night and we all agree. We are not moving. We're not going anywhere. Here is our home!"

Gloria continues. "We turn to talking about how we can make this place better. How can we make people pay attention to us? Out of these conversations came FANG. FANG does things for the Avenue. We do cook-outs and outings. When cellars flood, we clean out cellars. We get together to help one another. If people have problems, we help. We exchange babysitters. We get the street paved. We get new street lighting. We are able to do some off-street parking. The street sweepers come. We get rid of the junk cars. We make such wonderful changes on Franklin Ave. that it is unbelievable. It is the neighbors at their best all supporting one another. We have the support of the then mayor, Larry Bretta. We invite him to our cook outs. There are probably 75 votes. Hey, 75 votes. That is our first introduction to politics, realizing that community organizing can make a difference. When people in other parts of East Somerville see our success, they say 'hey, why can't we do that on our street.' That led to the formation of East Somerville Citizens for Action (ESCA)." [17]

Gloria explains. "In 1966 ESCA starts. The local settlement house, Elizabeth Peabody House, under the leadership of Walter Benecke, funds a store front to house the new civic organization. ESCA will become the flagship for neighborhood based organizations in the city. By the late 1960s and early 1970s it wields considerable power on behalf of the neighborhood residents. To the politicians, ESCA can mobilize *votes*. And votes were the kind of power that mattered more than money—the currency of politics that drove most officeholders. ESCA becomes a model for neighborhood organizations in the other poverty wards—MHTA, the Mystic Housing Tenant's Association, and WTCA, the Ward Two Civic Association. And the neighborhood associations become an easy entry place for neighborhood residents to make the transition from bitching about problems and unresponsive government to doing something to solve their problems."

"Fran Caruso, an East Somerville mother, becomes a director of the city's anti-poverty organization and, later, my secretary when I headed the Mayor's Funding and Development office," I remember.

Fran tells her story. "ESCA decides it needs staff. My friend Louise DiNucci and I volunteer. Then, we got a stipend from Peabody House. I get involved because my kids are growing up and I need to do something for me after all the years of raising eight kids. I was an only child. And I had been very shy and quiet until my husband volunteered me to be den leader for Cub Scouts–10 dens and 100 Cub Scouts. In those days a woman can't be a den mother, so my husband is really the leader, but everyone knows this isn't something he could do. It is a joy to me to have something on my own. That is my beginning."

"I came to Somerville as a bride when we first got married in 1944," Fran continues. "John was in the service in Europe. My parents bought this house and we moved here from East Boston. My husband came back in 1946. My last child was born in 1959. So by mid 60s the nest is empty. Organizing at ESCA happened because I felt I need to give something back. It is easy, just an extension of what I've been doing with the Cub Scouts. When I need to organize something for ESCA I have a list of all the Cub Scout families and they are all great. I love it." [18]

"The East Somerville neighborhood has strong self-interest reasons for supporting a neighborhood organization. Many of the families there had been displaced by Boston's West End urban renewal a few years earlier. They are just settling in to new lives in East Somerville when the state announces that it would build an interstate highway ramp through their neighborhood. But there is more. East Somerville is declared a blighted area and local government plans arouse neighborhood fears of more urban removal. ESCA grows and before long receives grants from a new federal anti-poverty program Volunteers in Service to America (VISTA). VISTA is a precursor to the Americore program begun in the 1990s." Fran Caruso comments. "We are the first VISTA volunteers in the city. Later, in the late 1960s and early 1970s I become a VISTA leader. It becomes possible to secure VISTA workers for Full Circle, the alternative high school that community people had started for drop outs. Full Circle has no money. I get other East Somerville mothers, Agnes Tiberi and Jean Collins, as VISTAs for the multi-service center started after so many civic leaders moved into city hall. I also get a VISTA volunteer working for the Shelter program for the homeless. As a VISTA, I chose to work on education. I decide to start a tutoring program. I recruit volunteers from Harvard. One was Pete Smith, whose father was governor of Vermont. He became director of tutoring program–and worked for no money." [19]

I interrupt the story to insert a personal comment to my club car audience. "What's amazing about this Somerville story is that as each individual took initiative to help the larger community, some became able in ways they never thought possible, others were energized by 'doing something real'–something far from the text books and far from the job routines they knew. The whole community came alive in ways that can't really be described. We had a 40th reunion of the Mayor's Inauguration not long ago, and many who came still claim these years as among the most relevant of their lives. This is change—positive unimagined change! But so often we miss its value because it's the accumulated nickels and dimes that enable it to be sustained; it's not a one day 'hit' on the front page, a headline in the *New York Times.*"

Back to the Somerville story. Even the church establishment is locked in the status quo, unresponsive and unimaginative about solving the problems facing the people within parishes. Church hierarchy and the Latin liturgy have become ends in themselves; it isn't permitted to see that the message of the preaching has anything to do with real life in the streets. Fran Caruso describes her first experience winning a battle with intransigent church leadership, "I got flack from Msgr. Hogan about my assigning the eighth graders as tutors. I told the nuns that student tutors would also learn. They didn't need to be 'A' students. It took a lot of effort. Finally the Sister Superior talked the Pastor into it. [20] Things became somewhat easier later after the new young curate, Fr. James Bretta, was assigned to St. Benedicts. Many of the '60s priests saw things quite differently from the entrenched leadership and life in the institutional church wasn't easy for them."

"By the late 1960s ESCA takes new strides. "We had Harvard students doing research for us on the proposed new school that we wanted to be built as a 'community' school," Fran Caruso continues. They get information on the background of various architects, and on school design options. We support Louise DiNucci, the other ESCA VISTA volunteer, in founding an Elderly Center. EMOC, the anti-poverty agency, gives us the money for staffing and program. Other ESCA members, Delores LaPiana, Mary Connor and Jean Collins get involved with health issues. They help found the East Somerville Health

Clinic. They convince Somerville Hospital to provide some of the support. And eventually, they are able to build a new building for the clinic."

While East Somerville was coming to life, Dorothea Hover, a nurse and old college friend, and I started Winter Hill Cooperative Nursery School. One of our first participants, Pat LaColla, recalls a day in 1966, "You had an article in the *Somerville Journal* asking for parents interested in starting as nursery school." (We just sent articles to the paper; they printed most of them. Silly that so many people had been intimidated about calling the media; they're supposed to report on our community.) "I call. We enroll Michael because there wasn't anyone else for him to play with when the kids were in school. You'd set it up so that parents could pay by the week and it's affordable because we all helped with the school, just need money to pay the teacher. That minister at the Methodist church gave the basement. We all painted to get it ready. We got stuff from here and there. The city almost refused to license it because there was only one toilet. The nursery school, that's where the whole civic thing starts. It is about the kids, right!!" [21]

Winter Hill Nursery was designed to accomplish as much for the parents as it did for the kids. The model revolved around hiring a professional teacher, but we insist that a parent contribute some time to making school policy and carrying out school programs. The motive is to graduate each year, not only a set of kids better equipped for the public school system, but to graduate a set of self-confident parents whose expectation for education is that, of course, teachers will respect them and listen to them and want their help. Official Somerville kept most parents some distance from school policymaking. Parents were expected to take the word of teachers and school authorities as gospel. Too many parents were intimidated; that had to change.

Pat LaColla and her friends set an example for the early reform movement with persistence and a creative sense of humor. She explained. "It's determination. It starts out with frustration. You get damn mad. You sit down and decide that instead of stamping your feet you'll start doing something. You start doing it. And eventually other people join in. I think the letters to the editor do more for me than anything. Seriously, if somebody knows that you're doing something and willing to put your name and address out there and say can we be in touch. You've never gone through something that other people haven't gone through ten times over. It's amazing when you bring up a subject, how many people want to get in a group to do something about it." [22]

Like others across the city, Pat and her husband Nick, become a force of their own. Among one of her many accomplishments, she recalls, "my kids had to go over the bridge on Broadway, that main street to get to school. When it snowed, the bridge wasn't shoveled and the kids would walk in the street with the buses, the trucks and all that traffic. That worries me. So I call City Hall. They said that had nothing to do with them. That had to do with the regional transportation authority, the MBTA who owned the bridge. So I call the MBTA. They said it had nothing to do with them, it had to do with the city. So I write a letter to the editor of the *Somerville Journal* and ask when the first child gets killed on the road, which agency will send the roses, the MBTA or the City. It didn't take too long once we got their attention. We got on the list for road construction and a few years later we got a new bridge." [23]

Pat recalls more of her adventures. "If you step off the edge of the planet and look to see the breadth of "reform"—a spirit to energize the Somerville population to improve the quality of life for themselves and their neighbors, you'll see something involving almost everyone except teens. But we needed to break free of the stereotype that all city kids either needed remedial programs of were delinquents. Many teens did need remedial programs thanks to the lack of outreach on the part of most school administrators, but the goal needed to be more hopeful. The institutional bureaucratic resistance to change made life difficult for Dan Macero, the one administrator with substantial vision for these kids. Dan is always helpful to our discussions."

"A group of local citizens begin to create a program that would provide an acceptable opportunity to get acquainted with the school administration and a program that can not be trapped by the bureaucracy because it will be a separate not-for-profit community program." Pat continues. "We begin the Community Ambassador Program through the Experiment in International Living. Such programs open new worlds for kids, but usually only for kids from well-off communities—because the alumni who launch local programs are usually without contacts across the class divide in working class or poverty communities. This scholarship will make it possible for kids from working families to visit the country of their ancestors, or anywhere that interests them. It is a way to make friends with the School Committee, the Superintendent, and the Administration. We'll all work together as the selection committee. Ultimately, we'll really make a difference in the life of a kid. And we'll demonstrate that new ideas can benefit the city. We just have to raise $800 to pay for the scholarship. We need a local committee. So we tap the people we knew."

Pat LaColla, from the nursery school, remembers, "The Community Ambassador Program I got interested in because I got dragged me into it. It was a damn good cause. It was. [24] I brought my friend Barbara Harkins to help solve the fundraising problem. She cooked spaghetti."

"I never cooked so much spaghetti in my life," recalls Barbara Harkins. [25] Barbara, the mother of five, and wife of a restaurant cook, was a born organizer. She had to be. Barbara also helps to solve another problem; all the new groups can't have the same leadership. So, Barbara is elected President of the Community Ambassador Program. "I got involved," Barbara recalls, "because I always wanted to travel and never could. Besides I need to get out of the house. I feel useful volunteering. For fifteen years I volunteered before I went to work when the newly elected reform group needed someone in City Hall to be office manager for the state mandated Rent Control office. You know, we really did something for those kids. One of my grandchildren's teachers got one of our scholarships." [26]

Barbara stops to note why it was all worthwhile. "What a thrill when Eugene Ferraro, our first scholarship winner, son of Italian immigrants, boards for his first airplane trip, crosses the ocean for the first time, and lives for the summer in the country from which his parents had come. And, all summer long, he wrote articles for the local newspaper describing his experience." [27]

"In 1966 and 1967 we'd started one activity after another. Most of them revolved around kids." Pat LaColla remembers,

"There is no place for the kids to go. The city owns a vacant lot
in Davis Square. We were arguing with Public Works about
cleaning it up. One day, we got 50 people with brooms and
pails. We called the newspaper, of course. We cleaned up the
grounds and told the kids to go play. Of course, it was in the
newspaper complete with pictures. The elected officials at City
Hall then designated the lot a playground. That's how things
change. A lot of elbow grease, some spunky local citizens, and
perhaps a bit of potential embarrassment for the government
that's not doing its job."

"And there was the Boy's and Girl's Club," inserts Nick,
Pat's husband. "When Michael and Danny were small kids and
I put a bunch of neighborhood kids into my VW wagon and
took them over to Tufts. I ask that the kids be allowed to use
the swimming pool. It took some talking, but eventually they
set a time for neighborhood use. That was the start of gathering
a group to found a Boy's and Girl's Club." Pat continues,
"Throughout the late 1960s' we argue with the veteran post
about using the old police station, where one of the post meets.
There was a letter to the newspaper about how inconsiderate
we were of the vets. The vets had done for us this that and the
other thing. I sit down with Barbara and we write a letter
back. It says that I have great respect for the vets since I have an
uncle who died in this war, a cousin who died in another war, a
husband who served in war. And, I have an uncle who was the
first to have his leg shot off. But that the Boys and Girls Club
is about something for all our kids. What more could they
say? Attitudes softened some. Finally, when Lester got elected,
we got the old police station to turn it into a Boys and Girls
Club." [28]

From these early beginnings in the mid-sixties, groups begin to grow. New people become involved and the leadership base expands.

For example, Jim Bretta describes his experience moving into East Somerville. "I went to St. Benedicts in 1968. It was a unique experience because I was assigned as a curate to my home town which was not the usual assignment for a priest. I had just finished my degree in Rome. At St. Benedicts, I was to work with a very old pastor who had not had good relationships with the assistants who had been there. His last two assistants just walked out on him. So Cardinal Cushing decided that since I knew the community it might be easier for me to live there. I was 26. The Pastor was 75. It was like living with your grandfather. Two totally different world views about everything. Everything."

Jim, with still a hint of anger about being trapped at St. Benedict's went on to say, "I became heavily involved in community issues because the pastor was such an egomaniacal son-of-a-bitch that he wouldn't allow me to do anything else. He was a one man show. He wanted you there at his beck and call to do the ritual kind of work. You were there to take an order and then go back to your room. So I go out to the community. It's a way out. In some ways, it's a way to keep my sanity And, philosophically and theologically, I believe very much that the church's ministry is in neighborhoods and around questions of justice and so I don't have any personal problems doing that kind of work. I grew up in Somerville. My uncle had been mayor for many years. I had a feel for the city and a sense that I want to do something good for it."

"There is a new neighborhood group–small but pretty active, ESCA–East Somerville Citizens for Action," Bretta continues. "They had rented a store front just down the street from the church. I walk in one day. Fran Caruso and Louise DiNucci were there–VISTA volunteers. At the time, city hall is looking at East Somerville as an urban renewal area. Nobody thought about the fact that many of these people had already been 'removed' from Boston's West End. Feelings were very very strong and right at the surface. Because of the protest from the neighborhood, the city backs off from their original plan and decides instead to apply for a concentrated code enforcement grant, the same thing by another name. They put together a map and highlighted by color what they considered the blighted properties. One third to one-half of East Somerville is to be wiped off the map. People get involved in the fight. We meet with the planner, the Mayor and the ward alderman who we think are not representing the neighborhood's interest. The community begins to think about running someone against the incumbent alderman in the upcoming 1969 election. ESCA crystallizes around the code enforcement issue and around electing another alderman."

"The community base (and the political base) begins to expand." Jim Bretta describes how local conversations grew into a civic movement. "People begin talking to neighbors. East Somerville, at that time, is a neighborhood and had neighborhoods within neighborhoods. People meet on a summer night sitting on their front porches. They get together for coffee on a Saturday morning. As people begin to hear other people expressing the same feelings they have, people begin to feel that there was some ability to do something to solve common problems. At that point in time, a lot of people are faithful church goers, active in St. Benedict's parish. They hear me saying that if you really profess to be a religious person you've got to get involved in these kind of neighborhood and community issues. That probably contributed somewhat to the growth of neighborhood activism. It took a real worsening situation, and it took communication between people to get people involved in making change," Bretta notes. [29]

In other parts of the city, the issue of kids continued to bring together individuals, who, for their own reasons, just happened to live in a neighborhood. One such individual was then Harvard graduate student, later School Committeewoman and State Representative Pat Jehlan.

Pat, now a State Senator, tells her story. "I moved to Somerville because I had enough money not to live at home while I went to graduate school. My family was from the suburban town of Newton. I'd done things as a kid in high school in the Methodist Youth Fellowship. When I was in college, Kennedy was president. People saw him as bringing change. My parents had been very active in civil rights and the peace movement. It was definite that I was intended to be like them. (I don't know that I would have said that to them.) I remember thinking to myself that I knew I was brought up to 'save the world,' but I couldn't figure out where I was supposed to start. I remember Civil Rights marches as very scary. The summer before I graduated from college, 1964, I went to Mexico to take part in a work camp. When I came back I heard about Mississippi summer and all the civil rights activity. You sort of identify with them. You think of yourself as being part of a very exciting time. I didn't know what to do after graduation from college. VISTA was something idealistic to do. I volunteer. It was the first year of VISTA. I spent a year out of state."

"When I moved to Somerville," Pat continued, "I had just finished my VISTA year and was starting graduate school at Harvard. I get involved in the McCarthy campaign. At the same time I was getting to know my neighbors. I meet Joan Sullivan and others from the McCarthy campaign. I meet some people just taking pies to each other. In 1968 there was some rock throwing going on in the neighborhood by kids in a local street gang. That leads people to talk to each other. WTCA-the Ward Two Civic association is started. WTCA works on starting a teen center. There is discussion about the plans for a proposed highway–the Inner Belt. It would really wipe out a lot of the housing in our neighborhood. (It's a different highway from the one that is threatening the East Somerville neighborhood.) Then there were those who didn't like the newcomers—us folks who hadn't grown up in Somerville. They would write to the newspaper that people hadn't saluted the flag or some such thing when their meeting started, so they must be communist."

"I think the first thing I did in Somerville was a volunteer project through the Ed School (Harvard Graduate School of Education) to help people in the ESCA plan the community school–in 1967." Pat recalls. "Later, I am the education chair at WTCA. And, when a group of people started the city-wide parents' organization, Citizens to Support Schools, it is natural for me to get involved." [30]

Quite by accident, the opportunity arose to tap the energies of these people and scores of others to create the critical base for city-wide civic revitalization. The reform movement galvanized and it turned political with an attempt to secure a school lunch program in late 1968.

"Starting such a lunch program," I comment, "had a number of benefits. It would make it possible for mothers to get jobs and increase the economic viability of their families. It would be a way to build public interest in educational reform without losing the support of parents who didn't feel qualified to address curriculum issues, but who all *knew* that their kids safety depended on what happened at lunch-time. Advocating a lunch program empowered people to act in their own civic self-interest, and was a really good thing for the kids."

"Reducing the kids time on the streets really was a safety issue," I continue. "Some five-year olds had to cross two major city streets and a railroad track at noon as well as at the beginning and end of the day to get to first grade. The B&M railroad has a freight train scheduled on that track just at the time the kids are crossing. To see the kids play 'chicken' with an on-coming train at the crossing really makes your heart jump into your mouth, The school principal at the Lowe School, the local school, is wary of parents from the time he had been spotlighted needing to accept the Sears Roebuck award for accepting into the school's (non-existent) library the racially diverse books given him by SRUC. Parents had had other altercations with him. For example, one day, a parent got tired of the kids throwing rocks on the playground at recess and bought a ball for the class. The ball is sent home with a note stating that 'ball playing is not allowed.' So parents have no reason to think that the principal would be supportive of the school lunch program idea."

When asked why no lunch program, the school principal and others in the School Administration answers: "'No hot water."

Disturbed by the answer, we form a group called
INTERCOM. Invitations are extended to all the people who
had been writing 'Letters to The Editor' to come together to
discuss citywide civic concerns starting with the condition of
the schools. Were these 28 old elementary schools were in worse
condition than parents had thought? It was decided to conduct
a survey of the physical plants. The School Administration
tells INTERCOM that the buildings are locked and that they
certainly can't allow entry to outsiders, not even mothers. Their
response only increases our determination to succeed. It wasn't
long before the local paper advertises that American Education
Week is approaching, and the School Department welcomes
the community to visit. INTERCOM decides to take up their
invitation. We assign two people to each school and they'll fill
out our questionnaire on school conditions. Mary Trant from
the anti-poverty agency agreed to take a leadership position.
Together with Pat LaColla they wrote a letter to the editor [31]
announcing that INTERCOM needed volunteers. A few of
the volunteers are university graduate students with out-of-
state license plates. (Somerville is a place where students from
Harvard, MIT and Tufts often come to find less expensive
housing.)

Who could have thought that going into the school with a
clip-board would cause the storm that it did?

"Outsiders." "Communists," principals charge. Phone calls
flew across the bureaucracy and everyone with a clipboard was
thrown out of the school—but not until they learn what they
need.

The *Boston Record American* wrote a scathing article titled
"(Mayor) Brennan, Board Lash 'Invaders' of Local Schools." [32]

We aren't outsiders. We aren't communists. We are mothers. But with this publicity calling attention to the school building conditions, our movement for civic reform grew exponentially.

"Do you know that one classroom in Ward Four even has a hole in the floor that goes through to the floor below?" One of the interviewers reported. Ward Four is where the largest public housing project is located. The local civic activity there, at the time, mostly involved Winnie Lawrence, the gregarious organizer of kids' activities, a couple nuns and Rev. Tom Welch, a young priest at the Catholic church adjacent to the project. (Only years later, once Lester Ralph was Mayor, did the activity turn to how the Housing Authority was misusing their resources contrary to the needs of the tenants.)

Others reported their school survey findings to the local paper. No toilet paper. Only cold water.

Despite the School Department's eviction, INTERCOM had gotten the information needed to prepare a report on extensive physical and maintenance deficiencies. We gave the report to the press. Barbara Harkins, INTERCOM president, received a much kinder headline from the *Sunday Herald Traveller.* [33] In its article "Somerville Parents Seek Better Schools," it cites our findings that there was a "city-wide absence of paper towels, soap, toilet paper (though money is appropriated for these items,) glass littered playgrounds, broken windows, leaky windows, poorly maintained heating systems and broken desks." The citizens of Somerville don't need advanced degrees to understand that their kids aren't being treated as they should be. No longer are they intimidated by the school administrators. Nothing can stop growing numbers of parents from taking charge of their civic lives because it is clearly inseparable from their family lives. The school building report is the talk of the city.

Pat LaColla, also involved in the building survey, comments, "Through the teachers at the Southern Junior High I know what is going on. That building is a disgrace. You'd think you were in a gambling joint. The teachers have those visors to shield their eyes from the glare of the dangling lights on cords. There are thousands of dollars worth of electrical equipment in the basement. It is equipment that the kids could be using. But it is all piled in the basement of the school because there are no plugs in the classrooms. My cousin Jim tells me. He's a teacher there. He says what he did was get five miles of extension cord and he pulls it down the hall from the office to his classroom. I write another Letter to Editor–an open letter to City Hall. I want them to know that if they enter Southern Junior High School and see a very tall thin man walking down the corridor with coils of rope over his shoulder, it isn't John Wayne. It's the French teacher looking for a plug so his students can use the audio-visual equipment in the basement. It isn't long after that before the electrician is at the Junior High School putting in plugs.

"The bottom line is YOU *CAN* FIGHT CITY HALL. If you're right, and you know you're right, and there's something to be done, stay with it. Stick to it. You'll get it done and you'll get an education on the way. I doesn't take money. I never had money to do what I've done. A reasonable request, a please and a thank you, can get it done. It doesn't take knowing what you're doing. We didn't know what we were doing to get what we wanted. We were too damn stupid. If we had ever known some of the problems that we were going to run into, we would have never started. When you start, you don't know what you're doing. Now, by the time one of these projects is over, I could qualify for a masters degree in half of these fields. If we started a project, we finished it. It would have been no fun, if you knew all the answers at the beginning." [34]

The activists in the East Somerville neighborhood became part of the city-wide school building effort. Jim Bretta describes their experiences. "In East Somerville we had the Prescott and the Hanscom Schools. I can't begin to tell you what the combined ages of those buildings were. I remember going into the Prescott and there was a sizeable hole in the floor in one of the classrooms there too. There were windows where it was colder inside than outside and water was streaming in. The city couldn't keep up with the maintenance and the city just threw its hands up in the air. It was that time–1968 the city had the "Marshall Report" done as preparation for the bidding on the design and construction of the new East Somerville Community School. That created a lot of interest. What is the school going to be like? How will it be designed? What kind of community access will there be? A number of different things coalesced. [35]

At the same time the new young teachers in the school system are also committed to the spirit of collegiality and hope prevalent in the 1960s. They bring new leadership to the Somerville Teachers Association and new convictions about how schools should work with parents. Eventually, the Teacher's Association (STA) becomes a critical factor in our winning the 1969 mayor's election. One of those young teachers, Maureen Amerol Hilliard, recalls "I was not political then. I start teaching in 1964, at the Prescott School, and by

1965 or 66 I am involved. Teachers win the right to collective bargaining and I am involved in the first contract negotiations. I get involved right off-the-bat in the Teachers' Association. I was on their board of directors.

"Maybe I got involved in the Teachers' Association because I have to have my own way. Those are the people who are the leaders. I'm the oldest child with two younger siblings. We were all brought up to understand that we were going to go to school which was not the norm. I'm the only one of all of my friends who went to college. I never questioned it. I am going to go. I am just always a leader. Stepping in and doing things is my norm. I am a student in a parochial school with a mother who is a protestant. They desperately needed help with 72 kids in my class, but they won't let my mother help the teacher, even though she was a teacher. Why? She's a protestant. Hearing and watching all these things have an affect on a kid."

"I remember the day of the INTERCOM school building survey." Maureen continues. "Where I taught, the principal put a chair in front of the door and said no parent will ever be allowed in the school. His misfortune was that he had four young teachers just out of school who were outspoken and thought he was insane to say that parents wouldn't be allowed in the school" [36]

Emerging civic leaders from across the city were so shocked by the school building survey events that they too increased their activism. Pat Jehlan recalls, "the first time I got involved city wide was when my friend Maureen Varney was part of the INTERCOM School building survey at the Perry School. She was locked out of the school! Those were pretty outrageous events. And, you, Carla, were just generating one organization after another." [37]

I had decided that we needed to counter the negatives of the school building survey with a positive organization that could be a substitute for the moribund PTAs and could become an advocacy group for after school programs and other educational opportunities. So we started Citizens to Support Schools (CSS). It was crucial to make clear that school reform meant changing more than just the buildings. We began a volunteer after school program for people of all ages. We filled the First Congregational Church with 200 people every week doing everything from examining snakes brought in by the Boston Museum of Science to learning from the Middlesex County Agricultural Service how to select children's underwear, to seeing films, knitting, and doing crafts and games. This volunteer pilot program led to securing a grant for a larger program and ultimately, CSS won a fierce battle with the custodial unions to open school buildings for after school programs. The group continued into the mid 1970s when its leaders, Pat Jehlan and Paul Duhamel, were elected to the School Committee. Fortunately, by then the United Church of Christ placed a full time staff person in the city. Paul Duhamel provided the staffing for Citizens to Support Schools (CSS) and also for the Somerville Corporation, our fledgling affordable housing entity. His leadership brought the resources that the community civic leaders needed to keep the civic movement going when, after 1970, the rest of us had become politicians.

The 'can do' spirit has been spreading. A dozen Letters to the Editor appear every week. Many of them with the tone of one written by ESCA's VISTA volunteer and local housewife Louise

DiNucci. [38] Her message to the political establishment is "too bad you are not involved in doing something constructive... instead of criticizing those who are trying."

Civic leaders were becoming increasingly sophisticated about how to win. Barbara Harkins remembers "If you want to criticize something, always put your statement in the form of a question. It invites discussion to keep the topic going. And it avoids accusations of slander." [39]

We discover talk radio. Disc jockey Tony Cennamo, at the local WCAS radio station, moderates a talk-show, taking calls and holding a never-ending public forum on what needs to be fixed. Barbara Harkins notes, "We'd call the radio in the morning. Tony always loves to get Patsy (Pat LaColla) because he knows he'll get a good conversation. We use WCAS radio as a forum to get information to the public. People would call in and argue. We'd call in with facts quoted from the school committee meeting minutes. By this time we were sending someone to monitor their meetings every week. We'd tell people how important and how effective community participation was. WCAS talk radio was very important for building a movement for change." [40] The ideals of Somerville's reformers can never become realities without the political support of a movement, and a movement will not be possible without using the media to communicate with the tens of thousands of city residents. Eventually, the station owners and management become nervous about the challenge to the status quo. They change the program format and the once proud radio station who touted itself as WCAS, the voice of Watertown, Cambridge, Arlington and Somerville, became a nostalgia music station. Tony lost his job. I later hired him in City Hall to help develop a citizen information and referral service.

The final act that solidified the resolve of many Somerville activists to move their civic concerns into the political arena began in 1969. John Cratsley, then a young attorney in the local Legal Aid office, now a judge, arranged to have Patricia Twigg from South Boston and me from Somerville testify before the U.S. Select Senate Committee on Nutrition and Human Needs in Washington, D.C. Stephen Rosenfeld, representing the Lawyers Committee for Civil Rights Under Law, had been influential in making possible these national hearings. [41]

I describe that event. "I'll never forget the conservative Mississippi Senator John Eastland, wanting to tweak Massachusetts Senator Ted Kennedy, asks me how it could be that so advanced a place as Massachusetts didn't have the most basic school lunch program that was commonplace in his state of Mississippi. I reply that some of those who run the city don't want to bother with new programs. Others, it has been rumored, don't want federal government auditors looking at city books. (Maybe, considering the *Boston Globe* 'Spotlight' articles that were to occur a few years later, those rumors were true.)"

Back in Somerville, home from Washington, the task is to turn the value of this widely publicized national event into something local that can help us get our school lunch program. Ellie Ellis, a Head Start mother, rallies scores of mothers from the anti-poverty program to meet with the Mayor in the Alderman's Chambers to discuss this Washington testimony. The Mayor agrees to meet. INTERCOM brought more people. And, even though I was not a Head Start mother, I was honored to be asked to be the spokesperson for the Head Start group.

We can't just report to Mayor Brennan; we need credibility that would put us on an even playing field with the Mayor. It's an election year, and, I figure, the Mayor needs to take us seriously. We've seen enough of polite, do nothing officials. Mothers usually get only smiles—if we weren't totally invisible to the decision makers.

So, I called Senator Kennedy's office in Washington. I asked if the Senator in his capacity as Chair of the Senate Select Committee on Nutrition and Human Needs would send me a telegram that I could read at our meeting with the Mayor. And, please send it to my house–not to City Hall.

The Aldermanic Chambers is jammed with mothers that mid-August day in 1969. The metropolitan Boston TV cameras are there. We sit at the horse shoe table facing the Mayor at the podium. Ellie Ellis, the spokesperson for the local Head Start mothers, presides. When it is my turn, I stand up and announce that I think Senator Kennedy's words will be more significant than mine in describing what his committee is doing. I read the following:

> Mrs. Johnston. Your concern about the health welfare of the children of Somerville is also my concern. As a member of the U.S. Select Committee on Nutrition and Human Needs I have studied the problems of feeding young children throughout the nation.
>
> Although Massachusetts leads the nation in the pursuit of academic achievements and technical competence, it has been made very clear from these studies that the Commonwealth lags far behind in its provision of adequate programs for feeding young school children.

It is my hope that your meeting today with Mayor James Brennan and other officials of Somerville will produce the precise results for insuring the provision of adequate nutrition for all of the town's children.

My office is always open to you, the citizens, to Mr. Mayor, his staff; and to everyone sincerely concerned about the ways to bring school lunches to Somerville's children. Please let me know of anything I can do to help.

With best regards. Edward M. Kennedy, USS.'

Mayor Brennan slammed his gavel into the microphone. The noise was like that of a bullet. Pieces flew across the room. He stomped out. The TV cameras caught it all. Wow.

Weeks later I was in line with my kids at the Dairy Queen. I heard two strangers talking, "Do you believe how the Mayor treated those mothers? All they wanted was school lunches. I'm not voting for Brennan."

Pat Jehlan contemplates the impact of the Mayor's treatment of the mothers. "To make change, you need to have an enemy. It helps if your enemy is not a marshmallow. It was very nice of the Mayor to break his gavel. If he had just absorbed you all, as a good politician could have, the momentum for making change might not have gained such speed. People act a lot out of anger. Also, 'being in the trenches with people' builds friendships. People become close and committed to keeping up the good fight. That encounter between the mothers and the Mayor affected the reform movement much the same way wars affect the camaraderie of the city's veteran's groups. We just strengthened our resolve and kept at it until we won." [42]

In September 1969, Mayor Brennan became the first incumbent mayor in the history of the city to lose a primary election.

WINNING CITY HALL: FROM PROGRAMS AND MOVEMENTS TO POLITICAL POWER

"Here's where it all comes together," I say to my train car colleagues—trapped in the Club Car with nothing to do but listen to my middle-of-the-night stories.

Mayor Brennan was not expected to lose the primary. No one took seriously the notion that a grass roots candidate could win. Even those of us riding the crest of '60s optimism and idealism weren't sure we could topple the entrenched politicians–at least not on our first try.

Since 1968, many of us had been flirting with politics as the method to bring about civic reform. It seems that the more we analyze how to fix what is wrong, the more we focus on politics. Government sets the tone for what was possible. Government has the power and the money to help. The wrong government uses that power and money to fatten the wallets of the greedy, the bigoted and the intransigent. We need to get directly involved in city affairs. One example of this shift began with a letter to the newspaper written by Gloria Albano's husband, Sal Albano, at night an organizer of East Somerville's Franklin Avenue Neighborhood Group (FANG) and during the day a teacher of retarded children. Sal began the 1969 election year with his call to citizens to "wake up and get involved in city affairs." [43]

Other reformers also became politicized. Pat LaColla describes one meeting at Western Junior High. "A sarcastic young man who is a candidate for something tells me to sit down and shut up. He says he doesn't need to listen to this. I say to him, 'I don't need you either, buddy. You need my vote. Now you sit down and you shut up and you listen to me.' I would *never* have said that years ago. Right. Those elected guys work for us. Our tax dollars pay them. We worked up to it gradually. It's like how I used to go into a doctor's office and be quiet. Now I think, I'm paying this son-of-a-bitch $75 an hour. He better listen to me.

"Once you start working on something and you see that it can work, it takes you to your next step and your next step. All the stuff for kids, education, special needs, etc., is so involved with politics. You learn. You get to know who has a say and who doesn't. You can walk into the teacher or the principal and you realize that each one has to go to a higher, and a higher authority. So you stop fooling around with the bottom boys and you finally learn to go to the top and aggravate the hell out of them because you're paying them and they are there to listen to you." [44]

On May 23, 1969, Joyce and Lester Ralph came over to my house for dinner. Joyce had participated in the Somerville Racial Understanding Committee and the Ralph children had enrolled in the Winter Hill Nursery School just a block away from the Episcopal church where he was rector. At dinner Lester asked me how the civic reform was going. He'd not been involved.

I replied, "we're at a point where we need someone to run for Mayor. Of course we can't win, but it would strengthen the base of the reform movement and publicize the social and economic issues that need attention."

"I'll run," Lester says.

Joyce kicked me under the table. I seize the moment. There isn't much time to think it through or to discuss it with others. I think that Lester seems the perfect candidate. As a member of the clergy, he had credibility. As a lawyer, he might know something about running a public corporation. His values, at least on civil rights, seemed to fit with ours. His roots were in a working family from Lynn—so the 'class' barrier wouldn't be too offensive even though he hadn't always lived in Somerville. The fact that he wasn't from Somerville freed him from any entangling alliances. His liabilities were that he didn't know anything about running a campaign and he was Protestant in a very Catholic city. It was already May and the primary election was in early September.

"Lester," I say, "I'll introduce you to my neighbor, Maris Vinovskis. Maybe he'll be your campaign treasurer." Maris, the Harvard student, has gotten involved in the Racial Understanding Committee. I am sure I can convince Maris to be Lester's campaign treasurer. Maris would be good for this job—organized, capable, eager to get involved in politics and as a Harvard graduate student, he was clearly independent from any questionable Somerville affiliations.

Vinovskis considered himself a liberal Republican, a member of the Ripon Society. However, he told local media that he disliked the tendency of many members of that group and of university people generally to get involved only in national policy debates. Vinovskis father had been a lawyer in Latvia. He was deported to Germany during World War II and brought his family to the United States in 1949 as displaced persons. Unable to get his legal credentials recognized by the American Bar, he went to work in a packing house and became an active member of his union." His interest in Somerville came as a result of the hard times he'd experienced as a child. [45]

Jim Brennan and Joe Marino were to have been the candidates in the 1969 race for the mayoral election–no dark horse candidate was even anticipated. Brennan's opposition, Joe Marino, was well financed and had begun campaigning months ahead. In late 1968, a new newspaper, *The Somerville Times*, was mailed free throughout the city. It named no publisher but, according to *Boston Globe* magazine writer Nicholas Basingstoke, "all the politically knowledgable people I talked to were sure that *The Times* was put out by the Marino organization." [46] The paper attacked Brennan at every opportunity. Other problems beset the Brennan administration. The State Bureau of Accounts ruled that Mayor Brennan "had juggled funds to keep the tax rate low in an election year. It ordered an $11.90 increase for Somerville."

Similarily, the Brennan campaign attacked Marino. An unnamed sponsor took out an ad in the paper every week showing a photo of Marino's elegant mansion in Winchester, a wealthy Boston suburb. The caption: "Why does Joe Marino want to move back to Somerville?" The political battle lines were sharply drawn between the two camps of old style pols.

The *Boston Globe* recalls. "At first, these (reform) groups were not too excited with Ralph. He had never taken part in their activities before, and anyway they didn't think they had a chance of winning. But he seemed like an honest person which was more than they were willing to say about the other two mayoral candidates." [47] Actually, our 40-50 activist civic leaders who had rallied around the city wide school building survey had created a movement that was about to take on a life of its own. These leaders mattered in that they are the catalyst for revitalizing government, but, they also are embarking upon something that, to be successful, needs to be beyond their control. In the last analysis, they are fortunate to have brought their movement to the right place at the right time.

The reform campaign quietly labors in the background. Maris Vinovskis makes a critical decision when he invited his new friend from the Somerville Republican City Committee to meet Lester Ralph. Twenty-five year old local teacher Robert Hilliard has been a government major at Boston State Teacher's College. Hilliard has helped in other campaigns, knows something about running a campaign and he becomes de-facto campaign manager. Hilliard says, "I'd spent some time in Republican politics beginning in 1968 and I worked in the Rockefeller campaign in Miami. I came back home to Somerville and I was teaching school. I helped out Republican State Committee who hired me to manage the campaign of a state representative who needed help to get reelected–but I've been a Democrat for years now. I met Lester at Maris's house."

"Lester and Maris were discussing some strategic issues, and. I was giving them my advice," comments Hilliard. "As it went along and I got more involved. You sort of had to make a blood oath with Lester. He said well maybe we shouldn't be saying so much about all this unless you're really going to be involved. I say, sure it would be a fun thing to do. It was June and the campaign would be during the summer.

"I helped organize his campaign. Lester was a terrible person to work for as a campaigner." Hiliard notes. "It was a campaign that had to grow over time. Lester always wanted instant organization and 50,000 house signs up the first week. He is not easy. But it is an interesting campaign. Maris, myself and Lester met a lot at Maris's apartment." [48]

Over the summer of 1969, the political ranks began to grow beyond the initial band of reformers. Hilliard gradually drew in the Teacher's Association. Uninvolved individuals across the city began to get involved. For example, Peter Bellini started calling his friends.

Bellini told the *Boston Globe* "I'm an Italo-American and a Roman Catholic and there was another Italo-American Roman Catholic running. But then I decide I am still an American citizen. There's so much junk going on, so much chicanery, that something has to be done." [49]

Lester Ralph has a different memory of the summer of 1969. "I'll always remember it as the most uncomfortable summer of my life...I was going through two or three suits a day. It was terribly muggy. But I met thousands of people." [50]

Hilliard thinks back, "That campaign was really an impossible dream. It was the perfect example of the right candidate at the right place at the right time. It never could have happened otherwise. The city had many bad experiences with many Mayors who promised to reform things and after a while it was just the same old thing. People got sick of it. The timing is perfect. You are running against an incumbent mayor who is unpopular. He has had some tax problems. And, he is running against a Clerk of Courts, Joe Marino, who has been removed from his job during the campaign for inappropriate actions. Marino spent a fortune on that campaign. And Jim Brennan just kept running ads showing Marino's Winchester suburban mansion."

"The great advantage of our position is that Brennan and Marino were ripping each other to shreds. We are ignored." Hilliard recalls. "By the time they take us seriously, it is too late. Whenever they pay attention to us at all, it is favorable because both candidates think that in the end, in a close race, we might be the deciding factor. Consequently, it is worth some of their effort to build us up. They just never had a chance to tear us down." [51]

Pat and Nick LaColla had also became active campaigners. "Somerville is just packed to the rim with a bunch of hoods and gangsters, says Pat. Nick qualifies it "Depends on who you mean." Pat goes on, "That's what it is, right. Then decent people come along who want to see things change. Lester stands for something decent. People who are sincere are willing to put in the time. Even if they fail, they want to try." [52]

Maureen Amerol Hilliard remembers, "By the time the '69 election came I was an officer in the Teacher's Association. Bob Hilliard convinced fellow teachers, Tony Fedele, Kevin Oliver, Dave Reilly and Frank Sestito to get on board Lester's campaign. Young people just completing their studies, people like Kevin Crowley, came onboard. They wanted people to organize wards. Hilliard had targeted the Teachers' Association to build the campaign." [53]   It is one of the smartest decisions the campaign made.

Then Jim Bretta thinks back. "I met Lester at the aniti-poverty agency sometime in early summer of 1969. We became friends. People saw Lester as a fresh face–someone not involved in politics before–someone who came with the label of 'reverend' in front of his name and all of those things. Symbols mean a lot. After the primary, Lester asked me if I'd serve in the administration if he won. I laughed. I didn't think he'd win. I didn't think the Archdiocese would give a priest permission to serve in City Hall. But when Lester won, I said OK I'll give it a shot. He and I went in and met with personnel board. They made a recommendation to Cardinal Cushing that he approved." [54] (This was an experiment for the Catholic Church. It was just before Fr. Robert Drinan's successful 1970 run for U.S. Congress in 1970.)

Throughout the campaign season in 1969 the civic reform programs continue to grow. Jim Bretta, civic activist Dominica Ruggiero, and I create The Somerville Corporation, a community development corporation modeled on the successful Cambridge Corporation in the adjacent city. The intent is to address the need for more affordable housing. This group provided the lightening rod for the only major attack by the political establishment on the civic reform campaign. In an effort to discredit us the Board of Aldermen objects to our incorporation papers on the grounds that "all Somerville residents should incorporate themselves so they too could beat taxes." [55] Since those of us on the governing board didn't live in low-income housing, had no intention of moving, and we were an all volunteer Board of Directors, that argument made no sense at all. But, then, logic usually is irrelevant in political bomb-tossing. We countered by drawing attention to the many successful efforts of the Cambridge Corporation, with its volunteer board, to provide low-income housing, refurbish recreation areas, and provide talent search programs for kids. Other than this one altercation between the reformers and the establishment, we spent our time campaigning and the establishment ignored us. Our fortune. Their miscalculation.

Marino is indicted for ticket fixing a few days before the election. Tensions are so high that those of us at the heart of the campaign took police advice and had a surrogate speak for Lester at the final campaign event–a rally in an East Somerville church hall. What's the point in encountering whoever was said to be packing a gun? I don't think we ever found out who was responsible for the timing of that criminal charge against Marino, or the backlash intended for the evening campaign event.

In November, 1969, S. Lester Ralph is elected mayor.

The Boston Globe reported, "It really CAN be done…an amateur reform candidate CAN be elected mayor of a big 'machine' city…witness Somerville, Mass., in 1969. White working people are usually thought to be supporters of the political status quo, bulwarks against the new winds of change coming from the campuses and affecting many richer areas…(Somerville) is 'one of the last refuges of the hack politician.'" [56]

Ralph's support is spread evenly across the city. He does only slightly better in the more middle class wards than in the poverty wards. He receives some 70% of the vote in a heavily Italian ward, against the Italian opposition.

When asked why they voted for Ralph and not Marino, one man comments, "If he (Marino's) spending so much money, he must owe a lot of people favors. Ralph isn't spending much, so he'll be free." [57]

Boston Globe reporter Nicholas Basingstoke wisely noted a comment made to him by Maris Vinovskis: "He told me to be careful not to overdo the importance of the campaign leadership. 'We didn't really do that much,' he said. 'This REALLY was the people's victory."

RUNNING CITY HALL

"Most people around here are afraid he is still an 18-year-old idealist who has no conception of how to run a $20 million corporation, which is Somerville." [58] This was the view the old timers had of the new administration. It wasn't true. But, it wasn't far from true.

That first Monday in January 1970 six of us move into our new offices in City Hall. None of us had run a $20 million corporation. All of us have credentials far removed from business administration. The Mayor is a clergyman and lawyer. Three of us were in executive positions in the Mayor's Office: Jim Bretta is a priest. Bob Hilliard is a school teacher. I am a young mother who had just completed my M.A. in theology. Fortunately Hazel O'Leary, the senior civil service staffer who Lester names as City Treasurer, had been the civil servant who had always run the treasurer's office for the politicians. Lester names Tim August as solicitor, who knew his way around both political camps—something of use. [58] The Auditor's position was filled independent of the mayoral term. (The Auditor was the point-person in the later *Boston Globe* "spotlight" articles and was the focal point of that unforgettable meeting the night the scandal was discussed with the citizenry.) Most of the Mayor's other initial appointments were teachers from the Teacher's Association: Frank Sestito, a high school teacher, became Commissioner of Public Works. Frank was older, knew the city well, and had a lot of political saavy. Dave Reilly left high school teaching to become Water and Sewer Superintendent. Kevin Oliver, a former elementary school teacher, ran the Highway Department. Bill Fothergill, a neighbor of Lester's who knew the building trades, became the Building Superintendent. A new mayor's appointments are critical (as is the case in any new administration) because they are the only authority for implementing the philosophy of the newly elected administration given the large and complex system of departments staffed by civil service workers whose job is to take direction from whomever the new leadership provides—even though they often would be just as happy to do what they always have done.

Our first task is snow removal. Jim Bretta recalls why it was so important. "I still to this day believe that the reason Jim Brennan lost the 1969 election was because voters remembered the two snow storms in March 1968. The streets weren't plowed. The sanitation department didn't pick up the rubbish for days. The streets were impassable. We weren't talking a record breaker like the blizzard of 1978. It was just a good Nor-easter. Jim Brennan's administration just couldn't handle the job. People remember." [59]

That first week of January, there were less than a dozen of us whose full time jobs were to make the new administration of this multi-million dollar corporation work. Fortunately, we had lots of friends who volunteered to help; but they all had full time jobs. University students volunteered by the score from neighboring Tufts, MIT and Harvard. The students were more flexible, but they were products of an education system that taught them to analyze problems and that the product was a position paper. We didn't need position papers. Our product needed to be plowed streets. We needed to prove that we *could* run a city. Or the honeymoon with the public would end within a week. We badly needed to keep the public's confidence. It was all we had. The weather was miserable. It snowed and snowed. Public Works mobilized the city plows and the contracted help. We divide the city into sectors and give each of our eager college students a map with directions to ride 'second' on the plow to make sure all the streets are covered and—more important—to make sure that the drivers lower the plow blades on each street. The civil service employees are ready to start a civil war. The students complain bitterly about how their major talent is in writing policy papers. We said, 'not now. Now, we need evidence that we can get a job done. You can write about it later.' The public was amazed. We kept their confidence.

The citizens across the city inundated the Mayor's Office with calls hoping for a responsive ear. In order to satisfy their need, Jim Bretta spent many hours solving problems—family problems as well as public service problems.

The political establishment is another story. They dug in their heels. They try everything to discredit us newcomers. Bob Hilliard comments. "We put up with a lot of bullshit from the old timers. We are branded leftists, communists, radicals. Our patriotism was questioned." Maureen remembers, "During first Memorial Day parade the photographer waited and waited until Lester put his arm down when everyone else was still saluting.

They ran *that* photo." Maureen Hilliard's voice raises in anger "Who are they to question anybody's patriotism? Those people took this community for 50 years and used it as their own political fiefdom. They raped it and took every dime. They have the nerve to speak about patriotism! What gall!" [60]

Most of the first term is a vicious fight for survival. Bob Hilliard is the mayor's office point person for that fight; his job is to deal with the various boards and departments–the internal elected and appointed establishment. He remembers, "We spent two years in the most vicious, most unbelievable war of attrition. It is constant. It is unending. It is not a pleasant experience. Very few politicians or community activists would have stood that for very long. We're fortunate that Lester's character is one shaped by persistence."

"We came in," Bob Hilliard continues, "every board, every committee and commission is controlled by people that are not friendly. Just getting our department heads approved by the Board of Aldermen is a battle. We really didn't know how to put a budget together. We learned that as we went along. We did our first contract negotiations and we gave more than we should have because we were inexperienced. You'd never get out of me now what the clerical workers got then. There was hostility. I remember being attacked by George Leavitt in a screaming match. He was crazy and threatening. It was a dangerous situation."

Hilliard continues. "The Board of Aldermen wouldn't vote for anything because they didn't want to give the Mayor credit for anything. The first term was fought over the issue of corruption. My time was so completely taken up by what had gone on before and the need to clean up the community. The

Globe 'Spotlight Series', Attorney General and District Attorney investigations, the resulting indictments are consuming of time and energy. By the end of 1971, the end of our first term in office, the election became a referendum over whether or not you wanted the city cleaned up. We said it in a simple ad. 'City Hall is not for sale anymore.' We won overwhelmingly against Marie Howe, a State Representative, who had never lost an election. It sent a message that we are real. We are staying. They'd have to deal with us for as long as we are there. We aren't an accident." [61]

Lester is a smart man. He'd made a clever decision by asking the three of us to staff the executive positions in the Mayor's office. Without a tenacious, stubborn, street saavy fighter like Bob, the Mayor would have been a loner unable to hold back the forces of greed that brought corruption into city politics. Without someone like Fr. Bretta, a native son with community credibility and a Catholic, he would have had to spend countless hours of his own time with the innumerable individuals who needed attention to redress problems obtaining city services. Jim also was a credible advocate for the community groups frequently filling a role as their advocate with city hall—a role crucial to keeping public support. And the Mayor needed a person on his staff who could create new programs and services, bring in the money to pay for them, and administer them as a catalyst to change establishment. That is my job.

As a woman, I am an oddity on the executive staff in a Mayor's office. No woman had ever had that job before. Frankly, that helped. My considerable success raising money is largely due to people throughout state and federal offices who are more helpful than they might otherwise have been.

I also reached out to neighboring universities to tap their intellectual and physical resources. The chasm between those who theorize about public policy problems and those who solve public policy problems is vast. I had a splendid time finding ways to link theory and practice especially during our second term in office when I am awarded an academic position as a Loeb Fellow in the Harvard urban planning program. One of the more successful university arrangements was when we provided a laboratory for MIT Urban Studies and Sloan School of Management students. One of them, Bruce Glabe, later became our city auditor after the auditor of *Globe* 'Spotlight' fame had been fired.

Julie Mack Davenport volunteered to organize and run a Little City Hall program.

"We have card tables in the business districts," Julie says, "asking citizens to file their complaints about city services. Our best results came from mobilizing volunteers to call block after block of residents, announcing that the Mayor's Office was calling to see if they had any unattended problems Had the garbage had been collected? Did the street lights work? The public, needless to say, is astonished that City Hall would call *them*. We had fun!"

We had begun the planning and paper work on the major projects like new buildings and infrastructure change, but such efforts require a long lead time and are largely invisible to a skeptical press for a year or more. And a skeptical press, quickly results in a skeptical public. So we plant trees where none had been for decades. Some federal summer recreation grants keep city kids occupied, maybe employed; we place the program within the Recreation Commission on the condition that they must expand their programs from the traditional boy's competitive sports programs and include arts, cultural and music events involving all kids in something we called 'Somerfest.' It is the first test of a strategy to change the status-quo by making offers that even the leaders of the status quo found impossible to resist. Slowly, we find the resources to refurbish city parks and playgrounds. To be sure, these programs are all a welcome addition, but mostly, in the heat of our first term in office, they bring the instant visibility that keeps the public behind us, while we buy time to undertake the more difficult changes.

State and Federal funds provide us an opportunity to operate without all the encumbrances of approvals from the recalcitrant Board of Aldermen. The money is not 'theirs.' I turned out proposals by the dozens. As the state and federal funds begin to flow, we focus on the human city as well as the bricks and mortar city. Traditional politicians usually focus almost exclusively on bricks and mortar. Such expenditures are good for commemorative plaques, for ribbon cutting ceremonies. But the bricks and mortar approach leads to a cynical public who becomes increasingly angry when told that their needs will be met with symbols. We focus on kids–a youth street worker program and help for the struggling Full Circle Alternative High School for drop-outs paid for with a return on our own federal tax payments. We focus on the many elderly left behind by families who fled to the affluence of the suburbs. We fund three Senior Drop-In Centers, created a Council on Aging, started meals-on wheels, started a surplus food program, and secured a state grant for one of only six model elder service Home Care Corporations. We focused on the unemployed. We put unemployed people to work with federal Emergency Employment funds. This 'make-jobs' money made it possible to create many of these programs never before possible and launched careers for people with talent but without opportunity.

For example, Pat Buckley, raising her two boys on welfare, has the insight and organizational ability to work with health professionals to oversee a reorganization of the Board of Health so that it was possible to provide more inoculation services and to fund the community health centers. At the end of the day, she got a professional job and permanently got off of welfare. She had the skills, just never the opportunity. Others followed that model.

We brought model police programs into the housing project and secured federal funds for a new communications system in the Police Department to enable both faster response time and the replacement of police officers on the switchboard with other operators.

The Mayor inherited a partially completed cable TV franchise. MIT students help us research all our options for utilizing this new technology to provide something other than a way for the cable company to rake in money from each residence in this densely populated city. We decide to insist that the cable company provide municipal government cable programming, programming of local school events, and a community access studio where anyone could learn to produce shows either to learn skills for future employment or for advancing involvement in civic affairs. Decades later, this local studio still exists and has created career starts and TV production opportunities for hundreds and hundreds.

Finally, after two years in office, during our second term, the big projects are realized. We finance construction of a new main branch library, build four new community schools, replacing buildings that are nearly a century old. We build the first new fire station in decades. We recover millions in back taxes. I represent the city on a transportation restudy for the inner cities of metropolitan Boston and succeed in getting a state agreement to bring the first subway stop into Somerville's Davis Square area. Somerville taxpayers had long paid taxes to support the metropolitan transit system with little service in return, yet Somerville's population, more transit dependent than the neighboring populations, had no subway stop. Doing all of this was exhausting, thrilling and unending. It took a talented and committed team working 24/7 to accomplish— with a lot of help from businesses and agencies external to the city.

Maureen Amerol Hilliard, the young school teacher turned Election Commissioner, identifies why we kept going. "Once we were there, we had to prove that we could run the city. There are so few of us holding this reform idea together. It is a bad time with seemingly unceasing veiled threats. The Police Chief even gave the Mayor canisters of mace that all of us in the administration carried for protection. But, we have a mission, (some would say a vision) to change the way business is done in the city. We work together to do that. The sense of community and the support of the community was what made it survive."

Maureen continues. "Part of what made it possible is that everyone, for the most part, is young and has no other responsibilities. Being in City Hall is your life–your entire life. It begins in the morning and lasts until one or two the following day. I don't know how people with children did it. Carla and the Mayor had little kids. But he had a wife. A couple of the other male appointees had older kids. At night we had board meetings. After that, you'd get a call from Lester to be at his house beginning at 11 PM and meet until 2 AM. The Mayor could be difficult—very moody. Bob Hilliard was a vicious in-fighter and that was important to have around in those days. Carla held her own creating and funding new programs. She and Bob met every morning in the Mayor's office. Each had different perspectives–both important—regarding how to solve the problems of the day. They'd have it out and the Mayor would decide. It was a useful process yielding a better result than would have been the case without the discussion. But sometimes it was nerve-wracking for all involved. Jim did an excellent job dealing with people from the community, solving their problems. All our disagreements were in-house. To the public and the Board of Aldermen we were a united group. And, in fact, *we were.* It wasn't a false team. It was real. [62]

I comment to my club car companions. "At first, the reform groups had a difficult period of switching leaders and learning how to deal with City Hall. After all, their history had mostly been confronting City Hall. One's friends don't work there. You're not supposed to trust government. The new administration lost some federal money because we took too long hammering out the new relationships for any urban renewal that wouldn't be the dreaded 'urban removal.' Sometimes, City Hall had to plead with the community not to carry out their plans. The Board of Aldermen, looking desperately for every opportunity to hurt the Mayor. So did the old guard still in Civil Service jobs. Before the Auditor was fired, his office refused to issue purchase orders for postage stamps to the Mayor's Office, for example."

Fortunately, the civic initiative instilled in the community during those early years in the 1960s continued, as it does today. Many individuals are unstoppable. Pat LaColla, whose activism started with the Winter Hill Nursery School, continues as an inspiration for the believers in self-government. She remembers. "I live on the little side street with a vacant lot at the end. Someone was going to build a paint warehouse on the lot, on our quiet residential street. I didn't know anything about this until the day they brought all this heavy machinery in. I go out. They thought I was nuts. I am in my pajamas, a bathrobe, my slippers and I took a beach chair. I just sat in front of the bulldozer on the lot. They call the police. The police come. I am ordered to move. I tell them I am not going to move. I tell somebody to call the television station. The television station comes. Then some state representative from Arlington comes down to find out what was going on—Eleanor Campobasso. I call Harvard and said I wanted a couple students to help me. I think Maris Vinovskis helped me with that. We did a title search and checked the Assessor's records. I got a book on all the laws for Somerville and I sat up all night reading it. I found a law from the early 1800s that it was against the law to take your wagon wheels over a sidewalk. So they couldn't take their construction vehicle wheels over to the lot. Let me tell you, that land is still a vacant lot! Thank God for a sense of humor. You don't need money and know how. You do need a sense of humor." [63]

"Lester came at just the right time," notes Gloria Albano. "Had we not had him to believe in, to be there, and to have hired a very good group of people, I don't think the city would have survived. There was a lot of disgrace about City Hall. We wanted to bring pride into the city. Why? For all the same reasons that we lived there and stayed there. We brought our children up there. Lester gave the city back its dignity."

"We were on a roll." Jim Bretta summarized. "It was a time that none of us should or could ever forget. It was a time in history that if we could have taken that model and made that happen in every city in America. Jesus, I'd feel like I was in the Land of Oz somewhere. People at that time weren't using their power for themselves; they were using it for the good of all and that's the difference. That's the difference! A lot of lives were changed because all these individuals made the difference."

Lester brought women into positions of prominence in government for the first time, and he made it more acceptable for men, as well as women, to be involved in advocating for kids. He included the local Black population at every level of activity. Tom Welch, a young priest from the parish where the largest housing project was located, became chair of the Housing Authority.

I added, "The Mayor's administration joined with transportation advocates across the region to "Bury I-93," one of several highways scheduled to slice this four square mile city, leaving less tax base and more suburban gas fumes. While too late to stop elevated I-93, the prominence of having a government join the citizens objections did lead to canceling the other two highways—the Inner Belt and the Route 2 Extension. I don't think the planners sequestered in their downtown offices knew what hit them when the Governor and the local Legislators unanimously insisted that the drawings for these roads be dropped—too destructive to people, to neighborhoods, and to local tax base. The citizenry had reason to believe that the government did represent their interests. From the smallest to the biggest problems to be solved, literally thousands of persons made this city work. Their nickel and dime activities made the kind of change that is very difficult to undo."

Jim Bretta looks back. "I believe this era really turned the city around. I just think that what happened made it much more difficult for the city to regress back to the kind of politics it had before Lester. Citizens group continue to surface and create themselves around issues as small as a tree being pruned to as large as rapid transit extension. Maybe there aren't the long term consistent groups that stay in place, but groups tend to come together–much more in this community than in others. Now, nearly fifty years later, folks from other places consider Somerville to be an active vibrant community. Somerville has always had the range of all kinds of peoples. The city is far more comfortable with that diversity than most suburban communities. And I think far more comfortable than even neighboring Cambridge. [64]

"My first story is over, gentlemen," I say to my train companions. "It was a time when some sunshine revealed the ugly underbelly of those who profit from exploitation and ignoring of normal taxpayers. It was a time when normal people became amazed at their own capabilities. They found initiative and courage. And fear did not deter them."

"Of all the individuals involved, special note must go to one," I say. "If Mayor Lester Ralph had not possessed his particular personality traits–being foolish enough to run for Mayor, being strong enough and smart enough to survive the fights, and being the person of vision, character and determination who enabled us all to make government to work, and for the sarcastic humor that kept us laughing, much of the change that was made would never have been completed or sustained."

I continue. "At the same time, the nickel and dime efforts undertaken by hundreds of ordinary citizens provide the fabric without which this remarkable story could not have been woven. So many of those involved will tell you that these were the best days of their lives—times when they felt that they mattered. And, as history shows, they did matter. They made change happen."

CHANGE MAKERS
Four Stories

First Story Notes:

The "nickel and dime" changes created by hundreds of individuals in the 1960s and 1970s that still have impact in the early 21st century:

- No pre-schools were available for working parents. New programs created 400 slots per year for kids. It spread to city-wide programs.
- No teen centers existed for kids hanging on corners. A $200k per year program for teen activity was started in four parts of city.
- No elderly social services existed. Three programs were started across the city.
- No school lunch program existed to provide nutrition, child safety on busy city streets, and the ability of working parents to know their children are supervised. A program was started for 5,000 children in 17 schools to receive school lunches. It became institutionalized.
- A deteriorating public housing project was a disaster. A building modernization program changed this situation.
- No effort had been made for the city to collaborate with others to maximize resources. New relationships resulted in government and private foundation grants to address everything from modernizing the police communication system, to funding conservation improvements, to bringing a subway stop to the metro-area's most transit dependent population. The city continues external participation.
- Virtually no racial integration was evident between the majority population and the small well-educated African American community. The new mayor welcomed racial integration in local leadership positions to as participants. Progress began.
- No women were involved in leadership roles in government. The new mayor made the commitment to having women as well as men involved in policy positions. Today, much progress has occurred.
- Poor access to health services existed. Three funded neighborhood clinics were formed including one that (by thirty years later) became a major regional health facility.

- No use of the emerging new technologies benefited the general population. The new administration negotiated a cable TV franchise that mandated a local production studio to provide coverage of local government, community activities, and school activities. It also provided on-the-job training for those who could eventually work in the television industry.
- Corrupt city government was accepted as inevitable. The new administration invited the media to do the research that resulted in the *Globe Spotlight Series* that enabled the reform government to move past the exploitation of three former city administrations. It also won a Pulitzer Prize for the *Boston Globe.*
- No new schools had been built in 15 years. Four new schools, plus other additions and renovations happened in this early 1970s period.
- No city involvement in regional transportation planning activity occurred even though three interstate roads were planned to cross this geographically constrained city. New administration and citizen involvement resulted in the cancellation of two of those road projects—the Inner Belt and the Route 2 to I-93 connector.
- No neighborhood enrichment activities existed. A funded "Community School Program" and a summer street festival called "Somerfest" were created.
- No letters to editor were found in newspapers. By the late 1960s and 1970s a dynamic citizen exchange was taking place.
- No sense existed that "government by the people" could be real. This changed. Somerville was given national recognition with the *All American City Award* for civic engagement based on establishing a community whose values and pride will, hopefully, never come from its white picket fences.

Counterpoint Two

City Government Change Requires Media,
Politics, and Substantial Public Support

The five of us in the AMTRAC club car see my 'making change' story from different perspectives.

John speaks first. "Don't you think the local government could have simply improved productivity, provided decent services, and cut spending waste simply by having some decent management? Run it like a business. Why would anyone go the route of all that involvement of common people? Housewives, poor people, kids, church people, school teachers. What a time-sink! Yes, at the end of the day, the city may be better run, but you sure did it the hard way." John, again, simply wanted us to know that "if we put folks in charge who knew what they were doing, there'd be no need for change."

John continues, "I work with public administrators all the time in negotiating development contracts. We send in our experts and help them if needed. But most of them just process the paper work in accord with acceptable standards for their region and it's a straight business deal. When a building is complete, taxpayers get to use it. What's all the commotion about?"

"But the paradigm is different from that of a development company," I say. "A development company's reward is to make the most money for the management and stockholders by completing a specific contract in the fastest least expensive way. Government has a different reward system. There are no profits—at least not legally–for the public servants running government. It's the public, not the company's management, that must be pleased. They're pleased when they feel that those who are paid to do the job get the job done right. People are sick of over-paying and being under-served. That's why they want change."

Paul chimes in. "What you say may be the text book answer, but I think there's plenty of profits for those running the government. Just look at what the *Boston Globe* "Spotlight Series" uncovered about the misuse of tax dollars. And those were 1970 dollars. Millions of taxpayer dollars were 'leaked' through in no-bid contracts just end-running laws for contract awards. Assessors were assessing the tax value of their own property and making huge profits in sales while finding ways to 'leak' tax dollars from the revenue base for providing services. Public officials were setting up their own businesses to insure government property from buildings to highway construction. All you hear is about the clever ways used to rip off the taxpayer and put money into the pocket of public officials. And I'll wager that a lot survive padding their own pockets because one doesn't hear about the methods they use. You don't hear about honest leaders. Do we have them anymore? No decent people want to get near government. And you wonder why we don't trust government? What good is top leadership if they aren't interested in public service, but only in their own self-interest—stealing? I think your whole story proves that despite all those citizen 'feel-good' activities, the underbelly of the system is rotten. And you wonder why I've given up and spend my time playing?"

Ted applauds the media. "Actually, your story was a great case study of how local media can be effective. I don't think that either local citizens seeking public services or reform-minded elected officials would ever have succeeded if it hadn't been for the accessibility of the print, radio and television media to follow stories and to do some really first class investigative journalism. That's why they call the media 'the fourth estate.'

Media's job, historically, have been to keep government honest in providing service to the citizenry for reasonable taxes."

Ted sits back for a minute. Then he continues. "The problem is that that was a half century ago. The media have changed. Mainstream media aren't local any more. And we all make our money on major entertainment—not news and public affairs. You'd think, with all the technologies available today, that it would be far easier to get information to people. But sometimes it's harder. There are very few decent investigative journalists, and they aren't given the time or resources to do their jobs like the *Boston Globe* 'Spotlight Team.'"

Ted elaborates. "All this new stuff—texting, twittering, email, social media, Face Book may make it harder to do what you did. We're playing with toys now. These toys can get a huge crowd to protest something; but I'm not sure we know how to use them to do the things you did? I don't think anyone's tried yet to harness today's media on an applied level to work through solutions to problems and to sustain a given civil society's new approach to operating its government. We deal in sound-bites and big splash 'scandals.'"

I comment, "the media today have amplified the 'gottcha game.' That's what government has come to be. Find a scandal, or invent one. Cut the coverage to minimize facts. Ignore the history. Fail to mention options for solutions. Don't discuss who has power to make decisions. Aren't there reward systems that can entice media to actually amplify stories and lead to civic problem solving? Or are we locked into the media using government to whip-lash the public from one hope to another to serve corporate profits? Surely, thoughtful people can utilize new media to solve some very serious problems locally, nationally, internationally? How can we 'make change at that level?"

No one answers. There's just the darkness outside the train windows with occasional street lights appearing and disappearing, The train is traveling pretty fast. There's that long whistle coming from the engine, we must be going through a crossing.

Richard hadn't said anything, but obviously was thinking about the Somerville story. "You know that story empowering countless ordinary individuals has several levels that are interesting. If I were still at the university, I'd tell my students not to dismiss it too quickly. Here's why. First, I think the huge base of public support is the ingredient that made it possible to turn nickel and dime change into more massive change that has been sustained for a half century. I doubt anything would last without both the level of detail and quantity of support. Second, I think communities today are no different than they were fifty years ago. People still want improved lives for their kids. They still get angry when they are ripped off. The only difference is that today things move on such a larger-than-life scale and with such glossed-over superficialities that individuals have a tougher time figuring out how to get a handle on making change. What opportunities exist?"

"The answer to dealing with today's discomfort felt by so many across the USA," Richard continues, "still lays within this nickel and dime change—this individual empowerment. I hope we can restore confidence in our communities, our nation's ability to be the force for good that it was in World War II. Our kids' futures depend on it. It's a real challenge, though. Even if we have today a John Kennedy or a Martin Luther King, Jr., who can inspire, they'll have a hard time being heard over the cacophony of noise called media. And there are so few local role models in how to be effective with nickel and dime change. Many of our brightest just say, forget the ordinary individual. Time is short. Just impose brilliant solutions from the top down. I think that's not workable; all you get is a quick PR flash. Nothing is sustained. And you can't make democracy function effectively without the 'demos,' the people."

"How about another story?" I ask. "This one has less ordinary individual input and plays out more within the policy tug between various government agencies. But at the end of the day, nickel and dime change happens and adds up to significant regional and national change."

"Still early yet," Paul says as he looks at his watch and then out the train window into the darkness.

"This kind of discussion is certainly not one I'd ordinarily have," John comments, but without protest.

"I think it's interesting." Ted says. "Some angles I hadn't thought about."

Richard leans back. "O.K., Carla, let's hear another example of change-making."

The Second Story—Boston Transit System's Run-Away Budget

Public Transportation: Making Change in One Big Bureaucracy

A NEW STATE LAW, NEW EXECUTIVE AND LEGISLATIVE
STAFF LEADERSHIP AND A STRATEGIC PLAN

"I'll have my coffee black with three sugars, please." The General Superintendent of Buses-Automotive Equipment entered the conference room and plunked his huge notebook on the table. A big football-player type guy wearing safety boots that make a lot of noise, it was hard to not notice him when he came in the room.

I didn't answer him. I had arrived a few minutes earlier. I am new and want to be sure I was in the right place and on time.

"Hey, Joe," says a skinny, wiry, all-energy older guy. "Wet out there today, huh?" He turns to me. "Oh, give me two creamers, no sugar." The Superintendent of Rail Maintenance sits down.

I smile and again said nothing.

A few more men come in. A tall man dressed in a suit, ready for work in an office rather than in one of the colder garages or maintenance facilities entered. He smiles and looked at the large briefcase next to my chair. "Going away for the weekend, dear?"

"No." I said and smiled.

Gradually people fill the chairs at this huge mahogany table. It's too wide to reach across, and long enough for ten people on each side. It is so polished that one could see their reflection. The chairs are sturdy, wide enough to accommodate the men with large frames who often sit in them. This is the altar of the MBTA. It is the Board Room where all the weighty decisions are made. The Recording Secretary for the Authority, made certain that everything was always exactly in its proper place before meetings began. At Board Meetings, her presence was required to take note of every comment in shorthand. She attends to all the details, but is not a participant in the discussion.

Today's meeting was not a Board Meeting. It was a meeting of the senior staff with their new Chairman.

It was 8 A.M. The Chairman walks in, just as the clock strikes. Bob Kiley hasn't been chairman for very long. Bob had recently left his previous job working for the CIA and accepted an offer from Massachusetts Governor Michael Dukakis to be the new head of the MBTA, the Eastern Massachusetts' public transportation system.

The state law has changed, eliminating the previous transit authority General Manager position and shifting the MBTA Chief Executive position to one reporting directly to the state Secretary of Transportation. This same new state law created the new Chief Budget Analyst for the legislative body—the 79 cities and towns that pay for all transit deficits on local property tax rolls.

The 79 municipalities were an uncommon lot, that is to say they frequently had little in common with each other than that they all disliked paying the deficit of the transit authority on their respective property tax roles. The big cities complained that service wasn't adequate because vehicles were not on schedule or because none were scheduled where some thought routes should exist. The very small towns wondered why they had to pay when they received very little service, or, for a few, no service. Many considered themselves sophisticated executives who understood running large corporations and that they were volunteering in their spare time to assume this appointment for their municipality. Some were more interested in the people they met with than with the substance of why they met. A block from the larger communities were full-time elected officials to whom the policy decisions at the MBTA Advisory Board made a difference to those scrutinizing them for voting yes or no on financial or service changes that mattered in their cities.

My job was to represent the Mayors and Selectmen. This was the first occasion for the senior MBTA staff to be introduced to what the new state law would mean to them.

The Chairman deposited himself and his large pile of papers at the head of the long conference table. He shook hands with me and said "Good Morning." He sorted the papers from his brief case and was ready.

He turned to the entire group of his department heads and said, "Let's get started. I know we all have a lot to do today."

The Governor chose well. The new Chairman has a very bright, round face, with a mischievous twinkle in his eye. He's well organized, well groomed, and clearly able to hold his own in corporate board rooms. He also employed his memorable Irish sense of humor with the guys, having a beer after work. But he was a no-nonsense guy. He was the perfect person to undertake this transition job, heading an authority that had had the same go-along, get-along good-ole-boy leadership for maybe three decades. He'd know how to 'talk their language,' but he knew how to command their respect, too. They'd try to give him a hard time at first; it's always tough to do something in a different way than it has been done for the past three decades. His job was to shape up the Authority and to get it working productively while keeping–or getting–his 6,000 employees committed to doing their jobs. The idea was that more productive management could increase ridership and stabilize costs while, over time, more diverse revenue sources were found.

"Agenda Item #1," said the Chairman. "Next Year's Budget Preparations."

He began. "As you all know, we have about six weeks to get the Authority Budget request ready to submit to the Mayor's and Selectman, i.e. the MBTA Advisory Board which has the final legislative authority to approve or reject our budget requests for the year beginning January 1.

"I need each department to assemble its data for me by three weeks from today. Our newly established internal Budget Office will then meet with you and with me. Out of those meetings, we will decide what will be in the MBTA's final budget submission.

"This year there will be some changes from the past.

"To that end, allow me to introduce you to the new MBTA Advisory Board Director of Budget Analysis—a position also mandated in the recent change of state law. *She* will review with you now the exact requirements for what you must submit with your draft internally and, as we modify it, the new information will also be delivered in the final document to the mayors and selectmen."

Jaws dropped. A few people squirmed and may have wished they could retract their coffee orders. (I could tell Chairman Kiley was watching this with amusement; he and I had been meeting for nearly a month now discussing how best to implement this new law and what each of us wanted given our respective positions.)

I'd been hired to be the Chief Budget Analysis Director for the 79 Mayors and Selectmen. It was just my kind of job. I loved meticulous research combined with on-site visits and conversations. I loved dealing with lots of variables and lots of personalities where it was necessary to figure out how best to do the analysis or assemble the pieces to bring constructive results. It was my kind of crossword puzzle.

I did my briefing and did not stay for the rest of the meeting.

I'd been studying the details of prior budget requests, examining staffing levels, reading what reports existed on service delivery for both bus and train routes. I decided that I should visit each department, each piece of real estate and let those in charge take me on a tour before I began the actual budget review.

"Sure, come Tuesday to see the Everett Orange Line Repair Facility," said the Superintendent.

"What would you like me to have ready for you?" he asked.

"I need to understand what you do, how you manage it, what it costs and what your challenges are. But, I am not asking for any particular reports at this time. I just want you to tell me what is important and back it up with appropriate documents."

"O.K., if that's it," the Superintendent said.

I'm thinking to myself, "I want to learn about the quality of his management as part of my tour and I want to hear what he sees as priority as well as what he may overlook. The best way to learn that is to give each department head free rein to tell me what they think matters. I will have many opportunities to ask questions and to pick up the documents. The tour will be my only 'first impression' time. Do they understand management? Do they take budgeting seriously? Do they think about performance levels? Do they hold their employees to any standards? What are their standards? Do they ever think about the customer who rides their vehicles? There is so much to learn."

Tuesday came.

"Nice to see you." said the Superintendent. "Do come in."

You could practically hear the 'click' in his head when he realized he'd forgotten something.

So he didn't sit down.

He used his body to fill the space between me and the wall behind him.

I knew immediately what his problem was, but decided to ignore it—with one exception.

As we talked, I moved a foot to the right.

He moved a foot to his left.

I moved a foot back to the left.

He moved a foot to his right.

I think to myself, "this is pretty funny. If he's going to be embarrassed by it, maybe he should be and there's nothing wrong with my helping his discomfort a bit."

This silent un-choreographed dance between us was worth a laugh. "Don't laugh out loud," I said to myself. Don't even smile."

Finally, he had to sit down and pretend that he didn't see me pretend not to notice the 'old boys' calendar on the wall behind his desk—the one with the naked woman. This was just the first of many offices that I visited with similar calendars. Some of the guys did better than others at not being embarrassed.

"Shit, I probably should have taken that off the wall before she got here," I can only imagine him thinking to himself. Why else would he be trying so hard to prevent my seeing it.

Of the Transportation Authority's 6,000 employees, at that time they had 500 women all of whom had secretarial jobs. Jane, the Executive Secretary, was the only woman in senior management quarters. I think there was one woman in the front office at the Everett Garage; but she apparently either kept to her own desk or the guys didn't care whether or not she'd notice the calendars in their offices.

"I don't know about all these changes here—a new no-nonsense CEO and a woman for budget analyst," the Superintendent may well have been thinking. "The new Chairman probably would look at the poster of the naked woman behind so many desks and either not notice it or admire it. But, this budget woman—I don't know. You're not supposed to have posters like this where women visit," the Superintendent may have been thinking. "My wife would be really angry if she knew."

As the Superintendent's mouth rattled off facts about the Orange Line, his feet continued to shuffle first left, then right, to keep in sync with my feet. His forehead was almost like a ticker-tape spewing out his thoughts.

"Damn, I hope she doesn't remember this poster in the office when she's critiquing my budget," he probably thought.

I'm thinking, "poor fellow. This is hilarious. It's O.K. if he has to think twice about his choice of art. After all, no one would think it appropriate to have a nude male over a woman's desk. But I wouldn't consider using his personal artistic judgment as a factor in reducing the money awarded to his department."

The whole game is, however, one more illustration of the real problem of the gear-shifting that comes with change. The

Superintendent may well be thinking, "New law. New people. New kinds of people. New ideas. What's a guy to do?"

The Governor and the Legislature had dropped some unavoidable 'change' in the laps of the MBTA's 6,000 individuals. To talk change or legislate it is one thing; but to be forced to live within a new paradigm is something that disturbs people's comfort level. That's a whole different matter. This institutional change had many more dimensions than one might immediately realize. It would take a little time to find the new 'normal.'

"We're on the tour now," I think to myself. "I'll just jump into the budget questions and we'll create the kind of norm here so he can forget the woman on the wall. That's extremely important if we are to establish the needed working relationship to get the best productivity for the Authority and the best price for the Mayors and Selectmen."

We moved on quickly to the grease pits, the row of Orange Line cars in for repair, the parts and supplies storage, and other key matters.

After about an hour he was telling me of his problems with the jurisdictional boundaries among the twenty-eight unions and how they often hindered getting a job done. He talked about the problems getting approvals on purchases from Arborway, where the Authority Treasurer-Controller's offices were located, more than ten miles away from this garage, and about the delays this caused to getting repairs done. He'd have to give the information to his secretary who would type out the forms, with carbon copies. Then someone would need to personally deliver them to Arborway. He told me that he had no idea what was going on at the Bennett Street Repair Facility, where all

Red Line vehicles were still repaired–until they moved to a new garage when the rail extension to Quincy was complete. He said it would be helpful if they could work together since they ran similar operations. He talked about the lack of inter-face with scheduling and how he'd get calls demanding that so many more vehicles be ready for use on a new schedule when he didn't have the people to do the work and was given no advance notice.

"I think he's beginning to see that part of this 'change' means that someone will listen to his situation. Clearly part of the Authority's problem has been that communication hasn't been what it should be," I think to myself.

"Good-bye," I said. "Thank you for the tour and for introducing me to your shop. I'll bear all this in mind when we review the budget submissions."

"Thank you for coming. I hope we can solve some of these problems," the Superintendent said. "Year after year nothing changes. No one listens. Same old grief. After a while you just settle in and clock your time, grateful that you have a paycheck on the government payroll. You know, the service we offer is really important to thousands of people, and to all those people who drive on less-congested roads because some commuters are on our trains. It would be nice to know that we wouldn't always get kicked around in the media, and that when we did something right people would care."

"It's going to take a lot of people working together to get things back on track," I say. "Thank you for your time."

"How did it go?" asked Eleanor, my right arm in our small Budget Analysis Office.

"After the first five minute adjustment to 'oh-my-god, it's a girl' the meeting went well. I learned a lot that will be useful to us, from people who I don't think anyone at a policy level has listened to for years."

"If in three years we can get a handle of the details enough to link performance and budget and know where the pressure points are that are critical to changing anything, that will be a major step forward," Eleanor observed.

"Get your hiking boots out," Eleanor said. "We have a date for your meeting with the Director of Operations to walk the approximately two miles of track from the Round House in Somerville across the rail bridge into North Station in Boston. That should be fascinating."

"I can hardly wait," I say. "All this data needs to connect to what's really happening out there, if it is ever to make sense. Otherwise, we'll be guessing from the data where to improve service and cut costs rather than assessing from combining the data with the actual operations."

The New Director of Operations is a rail buff—really a rail buff. He's also a Harvard Business School grad and the perfect person for the Chairman to have hired as Operations Director.

"Hi. I'm ready to go when you are," I announce. Fortunately, the New England weather was perfect on the day we scheduled for this walk. The sun was shining. The sky was blue. The air was brisk, but not freezing.

I wonder to myself. "Have other humans, other than perhaps the few who repair the tracks occasionally, ever walked this route? It's a wonderful route in that it is absolutely central to downtown Boston, but because it is only rail yards and track, no cars, no pedestrians, no buildings or homes, no access. It's apart from all the city noise and clutter. Of course, you have railroad yard noise; that's louder, but less frequent. I really love opportunities to be alone in the midst of chaos. It affords an opportunity to really observe, to reflect, to think and to plan."

"Let's go." he said as he gave directions to his secretary and closed the door to his office.

"I'm looking forward to this," he said. "I'm doing as much as I can of activity similar to what you are doing just now. I've ridden the length of all the rail lines and have gotten off at each of the stations. But this will be my first opportunity to walk these tracks from the Round House to North Station."

We hop the Orange Line to Sullivan station and then take a bus to get to the Round House. Both of us would have better held to our schedules if we had taken one of the Authority cars for business travel, but this afforded an opportunity to again observe what the Authority's and the Mayors' and Selectmens' customer base encounter when using the transit service. Probably one reason there's been so little change made in transit service in the past is because the policy level staff have no idea what's really happening.

"How long have you been waiting to get that light bulb changed," the Director asks the fare collector in the station. The poor fellow is sitting in his booth collecting payments for tokens people come to buy; but he's virtually in the dark.

"It's been a couple weeks now, sir. Thanks for asking." The fare collector said. "I reported it to my supervisor right away, but he's got to send it up the ladder and over to the other union, you know."

"Let me see if I can light a fire on this from the top and get some action for you," said the Director, making note of the location and problem.

One of the many problems facing the MBTA was the rigid work rules maintained by the twenty-eight unions. A worker could only do what was within his union's jurisdiction. People who collect fares do not change light bulbs and vice-versa.

"This is just one of the many bizarre work rules that hobble us from running effective public transportation," said the Director.

"You'll be pleased, in a few weeks," he continued, "to get an update from the new Director of Personnel. Of course, some of what he does can only be reported when new labor agreements are signed, but Dan will give you some sense of what we care about. He's been working with the Law Department and the labor negotiators to find ways to address the work-rule matter and a number of related items.

He continued. "The main problem the MBTA has with its unions is not how cumbersome negotiation is, but the problem with the arbitrators. The same group of arbitrators operates nationally. They travel from property to property ratcheting the wage scale up and calling their findings 'the middle' wage. The problem is that their loyalty is not to the taxpayers of any given region of the nation. It's to the industry. It may be necessary to change the law to effect the change we need in this area. That, of course, would be a year of fighting between legislators and national union leadership. This is just one more area for those of us who have come in on the wave of this State Law changing MBTA governance. But it will eventually need to be tackled to bring about lasting change in how business is done."

The Director of Operations is a bit of a loner, a creative guy who collects rail memorabilia and likes being out in the country and also in the heart of the city. He's unique in that he may be the only Harvard Business School graduate in recent years who has specialized in railroads. He's probably in his mid-30s. It's clear he relishes the challenge before him. If ever a bureaucracy needed dusting off and made relevant to current demands, the MBTA fit that bill. It's easy to tell that he found his job both fun and challenging. He liked to make change. To have individuals like that in positions where change is needed, the opportunity to make change happen greatly increases. No doubt, the Director was motivated for success. And one should never doubt that he succeeded.

We arrived at the Round House—an amazing, huge 19th century structure set on a significant number of acres of property at the southern tip of Somerville. The Boston and Maine Railroad Yard, once central to a rail transportation empire, would be prime real estate today in the late 20th century were it not already occupied.

The acreage, effectively off the local tax records for years (to the irritation of the city in which the property was located), reached to the edge of the Boston Harbor with the entry to the Charles River on one side and with the Mystic River not far from the other side of the parcel. A developers dream in the 20th century, the land was protected by a mix of railroad law, rail bankruptcy law, and now MBTA law.

One hundred years before it became a transportation hub, this land might well have been traversed by American colonists in the 18th century fighting for freedom from Great Britain. Forces engaged in the Battle of Bunker Hill, not much more than a mile northeast. When Paul Revere rode his horse from the Old North Church in Boston toward Lexington and Concord, had he crossed the water as the crow flies he might well have come across this parcel of land on the his route. Similarly, other colonists surely trooped through here when they raised the first American Flag on January 1, 1776 on Somerville's Prospect Hill, barely half-a-mile from where we now stand.

We meet with some of the employees and walk through the dimly lit, marginally used Round House. The Boston and Maine Railroad (B&M) isn't what it once was. Now the roundhouse land and commuter rail tracks belonged to the MBTA. The MBTA contracted with the railroad to run commuter rail service while the railroad continued its freight operation here and on other rights-of-way owned by the railroad.

"I remember visiting Mayors and Selectmen to lobby for the votes needed to purchase the B&M real estate and right-of-ways." I said to the Director. "What a milestone to have convinced the majority of the 79 municipalities to vote yes. A lot of people worked very hard—mostly totally below the media radar–on making this change happen."

For a long time, the MBTA had been hampered in offering public transportation service to those taxpayers who lived in suburbs and paid, but couldn't ride. And the bankrupt B&M wasn't doing much very well. This innovative plan would enable access to federal money available for restoring tracks and other facilities along right-of-ways. That was the first step toward operating commuter rail. By leasing the commuter service from the railroad, the MBTA accomplished several important objectives: 1) train service became available, 2) the B&M brought in some much needed revenue and 3) the employees running the service were not part of the MBTA and hence not part of any of the MBTA unions.

We set off on our walk along the tracks. "This is the main track into the city," the Director said. "I look forward to seeing this first hand; it's good to find an hour away from meetings and data crunching."

"Tell me how your priorities line up for capital dollars," I asked? "For example, some of these railroad ties look pretty loose. I don't know what the frequency of replacement is. If they need to be replaced, what pot of money must be used—local property tax money or federal capital money?"

"Good question." the Director replies. "You can imagine that with the miles of right-of-way we operate and the decades of no money, no riders and little effective governance, our maintenance problems need attention. We've completed a survey and are compiling the results now to identify exact problems. I look forward to its public release because I'm certain that some of the local public officials with rail experience as well as all those retired train advocates across metropolitan Boston will have some good comments for us."

What a unique walk. I'm absorbing every bit of what we see pertaining to the railroad, and adding my own frosting–the opportunity to walk where so few in this century have walked. I've tried to imagine what has happened on this land in the 1700s and 1800s.

We come to the trestle that carries the tracks across the river. Single file, Dave and I walk to the edge of the trestle mindful that a train may come through at any moment.

I think to myself, "I must be crazy to like this. And, he's as crazy as I am. I think he likes it, too. Maybe it's because we are both Aries—I think I'm right about that. I had heard that when his staff had a party for him. Some say that those with the astrological sign of Aires are always eager for adventure and creative. Hmmmm."

"Remember to stay as far from the track as there is room," the Director said. "The trains are wider than the track, you know."

I look to my left. There's open air and an occasional steel girder. I look to my right, There's track and space for a train. I look below me. Aside from the narrow wooden path on which I walk, it's pretty much just open.

I wonder silently. "If I fell off of this, I wonder if a person would still be alive after the impact on the river so far below. Of course, a person could miss the river and get impaled on one of the trestle legs or on a boat."

Not to show any concern, I comment, "golly, the condition of this trestle looks far worse than the rails."

"We've had people checking every joint in this ancient bridge. The rust and disrepair has concerned us greatly. Things have been neglected far too long." The Director continued. "An accident cannot be tolerated. Wouldn't it quickly bring an end to all that we are trying to do to turn the management around if a train went into the river because the bridge failed?"

"How terrible," I said. "An accident would be terrible in its own right, but the media would simplify it all into a witch hunt to run the new management out of town."

"That's how it often works these days," the Director commented. "I don't know why we as a nation are surprised when our public policy makers accomplish so little. Occasionally, people really do want to fix past problems. Occasionally, the right team of motivated people with the right skills, the right legal mandate, and sufficient resources to solve problems start to turn a ship around. But the public and the media are impatient, mostly because they have no idea of the details needed in order to accomplish major change. Lots of nickel-and-dime projects need to be completed before we make a lasting difference. It is possible to make that change if we're given reasonable time. But, in politics, a huge emotional explosion without any attention to the facts or the skills needed to correct problems usually results in running out of town the very people needed to correct what's wrong. Too bad no one cares about context or detail."

"A lot is about timing," I say. "The increased interest in public transportation, the new law, the particular interest from the Governor, the skill and self-interests of the new management team, and the commitment of the Mayors and Selectmen to push hard to keep costs manageable, and to do it without sacrificing the objective of upgraded service are all on the ball field at the same time. If we don't make too many mistakes and don't descend into unproductive fights, we can move this bureaucracy forward a half-century. I'd wager that it would take five or six years to codify new directions. But how's the public to really know whether this current set of so-called reformers is really any more skilled or committed than those who precede us. There's hardly a way for people to know that."

We're walking single file. I'm behind the Director. A train passed. Wow. Windy. The trestle shook. We were awfully close to the side of those box cars and to the edge of the trestle.

The Director turns around. He smiles. "You know it would be hard on the railroad workers compensation budget if the company didn't make the path we're on wide enough for a skinny employee and a train to pass each other. And the railroad is not interested in law suits, either."

"Whew." I said. "I'm fine. I probably would be finer if you'd reminded me earlier about the self-interest of the railroad in constructing the path wide enough so they wouldn't kill or maim too many employees."

We laugh.

We finished our walk, entered North Station and said good-bye. It was like walking from one world into another to leave the railroad property and emerge into a busy station full of people, fast food places, kids screaming and all that most people consider 'normal' while they get on or off a bus or train, simply taking for granted that all will run as it should.

One aspect of the budget that we wanted to get a handle on as result of these site visits was how productivity in service delivery interconnected with the budget decisions.

"How could I not have seen it before?" I say to Eleanor upon my return the following week from visiting the Reservoir repair facility for Green Line vehicles.

"What's that?" Eleanor asks. I'm so fortunate to have Eleanor as my chief assistant. This petite, spectacled woman is about sixty. She's never had a job like this before. But she has all the skill required and her enthusiasm about being in a professional job position, plus her excitement about doing something that might result in public service improvements, keeps her very productive.

"I finally realized why Reservoir has such a poor record for completing repairs on vehicles to supply the fleet to meet the schedule for running service," I said. "It's so simple."

"When no top management pays attention to what's happening over the years," I responded, "the clock ticks on providing promotions, and then the crackdown says that there are no new dollars for new hires, and you end up in more than a mess. You end up with a major repair shop full of foremen and very few workmen."

"So no one worked on the repairs over the years." Eleanor says.

"Ah, but lots of experts weigh in to comment on what needs to be repaired." I laugh.

"And the ripple effect?"

"First, the Green Line operations people yell and scream at the garage people for not getting their job done. They get sick of listening, so they turn up the volume on their music and ignore it all." I continue. "Second, everyone grinds to a halt. The major accomplishment of the day is punching the time clock in the morning and punching it again when one leaves in the afternoon. You can't blame them really. The workers in the garage feel over-worked and over-supervised. The foremen in the shop will be reprimanded by the union if they do something that is not in their job description, and, besides, it would be demeaning to do the job they'd moved up from. The Green Line people trying to meet a schedule have to keep the head-ways and have very little time to figure out why Reservoir isn't performing. It's not their job to figure that out and even if they did find out, there's nothing they could do that wouldn't aggravate things more."

"That's how we got into the crisis that prompted the new state law," I said. Everyone assumed nothing could be done. Nothing ever changed. No one at a policy level even had a clue about these nickel and dime problems. They were all absorbed in the cosmic problems that require endless discussion with their peers and the people who keep the financial and management gears turning."

"Here's where we can come in," Eleanor says.

"You're right, Eleanor. As we get past this first year, I intend to expand our budget report to one that includes productivity and service delivery issues. I think we can do that. It's more work for us but it will be satisfying to do."

I look at the calendar. Tomorrow is the visit I saved for last," I say. "I go to Arborway to meet with the Treasurer-Controller and his department."

The Arborway office building of the MBTA once housed all the administrative offices. That was before the Chairman and Board as well as all who needed day-to-day contact with key business and government offices in the center of Boston moved back from this idyllic suburban location to where one could walk among the downtown offices. From Arborway it took thirty to forty-five minutes to reach the city center. For now, the General Counsel and the Treasurer-Controller remained at Arborway.

"The boss's office is over there," a helpful employee directed when we entered the Treasurer-Controller's department.

I walked past rows of desks in a huge room to the corner office.

"Hi. Nice to see you," said the Treasurer-Controller. "I hear you've been to every piece of real estate on the Authority's books."

"And now I'm here to see you and to have you give me a tour of your department," I said.

"Things certainly are different this year," the Treasurer-Controller said. "Every year, we pull together the budget submission for the Mayors and Selectmen. As soon as the General Manager—woops, I mean the Chairman, the job's new name–approves the numbers I pull the request together and he sends it over to your Board. It's just the one page summary of line items with maybe a page or two highlighting anything special. If your Budget Committee has any questions, they call the guy on the regional planning council staff who deals with transportation. He comes over to meet with me and I answer his questions. That's always been pretty easy. So, What's the big deal?"

The Treasurer-Controller waited a moment to judge my reaction. I gave no reaction. He continues. "After all, the Revenue is what it is. We just count it. The Expenditures are basically fixed. Most of that's wages and fringes and you can't do much there because of the union contracts. We have no control over whether or not the Accident and Sickness Insurance or Health Insurance or Workmen's Compensation Insurance line items increase from year to year. The Fixed Charges don't change once the bond issues are floated. Fuel costs increase, but we have no control there. So, what's the big deal?"

He stopped again to let his point sink in—unhappy that I made no comment and showed no response.

"Now the new Chairman has set up his own Office of Budget and Operations Analysis. And it's down at High Street, part of the Chairman's Executive Office. He's doing his own internal review of financial management. And, then, you're here representing the Mayors and Selectmen and you are insisting that the departments provide even more added information."

He didn't say it, but I can imagine that he was thinking to himself, "and you're visiting every department, every maintenance shop and making everyone nervous with all the questions."

I said quietly, "it's nice of you to show me through your department today. You've watched this new law develop longer than I have. I think it's pretty clear that the Mayors and Selectmen across all of Eastern Massachusetts and the State Legislature and the Governor all feel that the MBTA deficit has grown much too rapidly and that the budget seems simply to run away with Supplemental after Supplemental following the annual submission. All the attention you're getting is focused around learning how we can provide more public transportation service to more of the public at costs that are much more reasonable."

"Well, you can't do much about the dollars unless you drastically cut service," the Treasurer-Controller said. "But let's start our tour."

We start walking through the department past desk after desk. The books say that this department has 185 people on staff.

I think to myself, "I know he's dealing with roughly $244 million in operating budget plus the capital budget of about $290 million expenditures on bond proceeds. I'll need to research the financial management in more detail, but I wonder if well-run private corporations of this size have 185 people handling their investments, accounts, transactions and audits? Some of the other MBTA departments with comparable work load have far fewer employees."

We walk.

"You know that in recent years we've had to add more auditing capability to meet the accountability requirements for the federal grants," he said. We didn't used to get grants for public transportation capital projects. All that money used to just go to highway construction. It's nice to be able to expand and modernize, but it sure is a pain in the neck to have to fill out their reports and respond to their audits. They try to keep a short leash on what we do with that grant money." The Treasurer-Controller moves rapidly from one part of his department to another, not slowing down enough for any conversations to start with other employees.

"The new Chairman is putting in place a new revenue collection system," he said. For decades we've had a system of collecting from each toll booth across the entire system and each bus fare box. We'd do it mostly in the middle of the night after the system shut down at 2 A.M. so that we could tally one day's receipts and start fresh when the system opened at 5 A.M. It used to all be collected and taken to a central processing place for our employees who worked in revenue collection. Now the Chairman is gradually instituting this vacuum system, as soon as the equipment can be installed. It mechanically extracts the revenue from the fare box and places it directly into high security containers that are delivered directly to the bank."

I think to myself, "About time. It will be interesting to see the difference in the data tallying revenue collected. So easy. So tempting for boxes full of coins to just lose a pile of quarters. Surely few people would steal; let's give employees the benefit of the doubt. But why leave this all to temptation? I'll bet that there are a lot of reasons why this department isn't pleased with the changes taking place."

The Treasurer-Controller takes a minute to answer someone's question. So I strike up a conversation with a man at a nearby desk.

"Hi, I'm Joe." He said. "I've heard about you and the new Mayors' and Selectmans' budget process. Hell, everybody's heard about you. News travels fast about which office you visit and what you ask."

"How long have you been working in the Treasurer's Office, Joe?"

"Me? I started here when I got out of high school in 1930. Been here ever since. I guess that's a bit over forty years."

"Jack, how long you been here?" Joe asks the guy at the next desk about 5 feet away.

"Same time. I graduated the year after you, Joe, remember?"

Joe explains, "You see, those were the depression years. If you were lucky enough to get a job in those years, you held tight. You never thought about changing jobs!"

"That's what I've heard from lots of people. Lucky to find a job in the 1930s," I said.

Jack fills in. "You see most of us have been here in this same job, in this same room for forty years. We know each other real well. Our families have known each other since we were all school kids. You should see us play baseball. We have our own team."

Jack and Joe chat on, telling stories about 'the good old days.' I listen and smile. But I'm thinking to myself. "This department is the heart beat of the Authority, the money management; but it's more than that. This department is a family, a place where the same bureaucrats meet day-after-day for their entire working career. It's comfort and security to them. What effect does that have on the skillful and productive management of the department's business?"

I carry my thought forward. "The cohesiveness of this gang of guys must be a nice thing in our crazy and chaotic society. That could result in a team effort that makes things function more smoothly. On the other hand, that could also result in only minimal business being done because there are so many other things to talk about—family gatherings, baseball, kids, illnesses. Just the very act of the new Executive and Legislative management trooping through their work space, asking questions, making changes must be un-nerving, a threat to business-as-usual. The trick of making effective change, change that takes root and lasts, requires getting key leaders on-board from the 'old guard' so that it's possible for the bulk of the workers to embrace the changes. Otherwise, change won't work. Too much time loss and too much disruption will sabotage efforts to change. We will have simply stirred up a hornet's nest and not accomplished anything that can be codified and sustained."

I hear John calling.

"Ready to go?" the Treasurer-Controller asks.

"Yes," I responded. "This has been very helpful. Indeed, budget analysis is about number crunching, but not everything that needs to be factored in appears on a piece of paper."

"That certainly is the case. I've managed this department for a couple of decades, now. Anyone new will learn the hard way if they aren't interested in hearing about why we do what we do. Thanks for your questions. I hope I've answered them. You have my phone number if you need anything else." John and I shake hands and I leave.

Back in town, I drop by our office to leave some papers.

"Hello, Eleanor."

"How was the Arborway tour?" she asked.

"Do you remember that fellow who dropped into the office last week? He was talking about how his city was setting up an affirmative action office because local citizens had complained about city hiring."

"How can I forget him?" Eleanor said. "His quip about the MBTA will stick with me for a long time. Remember? He said that affirmative action for the MBTA would be hiring white male Italians."

"Exactly." I said. "Today certainly painted the picture of what he meant. On the one hand, he couldn't be more right. On the other hand, doesn't a company really need a cohesive group of employees who understand their mission and who have the skill and motivation to work together to get the job accomplished? The trick is to make that focus around people's skill and work ethic and personality—whatever their demographic description may be."

"True," Eleanor said. "as long as you don't systematically exclude any one segment of individuals who have what it takes to do the job, but who aren't allowed in the door because of their demographic profile."

"Right. I'm going home," I say. "We switch gears now and start assembling and analyzing all this material to prepare our annual budget report for the Mayors and Selectmen. Let's see what comes of it."

"Good Night."

"So, my fellow Club Car companions," I say, "this was the beginning of efforts to make change in one of the largest, most costly bureaucracies within Massachusetts government. You have heard some of the tales from the first year of operating within the new state law with carefully selected individuals to take on each role deemed crucial to implementing the mandated change."

I continue to fill in my club car companions. "What you haven't heard in any detail is that the Mayors and Selectmen hired their Chief Budget Analyst a good nine months before the new Chairman arrived to run the Executive Branch. This made it possible for the Legislative arm of the MBTA, the MBTA Advisory Board, which wasn't advisory, but had final authority on setting budgets, to complete a thorough reference volume on the existing situation at the MBTA—one that, from the viewpoint of the Mayors and Selectmen, reflected the situation of service delivery, productivity, cost effectiveness, and management. The Chief Budget Analyst of the MBTA Advisory Board then briefed the new Chairman prior to his actual arrival at the Authority."

"It was a clever plan created by those in the Governor's Office and the key Mayors and Selectmen on the Advisory Board's Executive Committee called 'The Budget Committee.'" I note. "It jump-started creating the kind of change that had some hope of working. It enabled the new Chairman to know some of what he would encounter before he began work. It enabled the Mayors and Selectmen and their new Budget Analysis Director to be heard by the Chairman; they were able to clearly articulate the problems facing those who paid the deficit and got complaints about poor service. And it enabled both the new Chairman and the new Director of Budget Analysis, those filling the key Executive and Legislative jobs, to work together, to learn to listen to each other, and to respect each other with common objective in focus—good grounding for the fact that as time passed there would be many situations where they were required to take adversarial roles." [1]

"It's not easy to implement viable sustained change in an institution as large and as entrenched as the MBTA. The last part of my story," I say "jumps ahead to the third year of this new experiment. The small Advisory Board Office is completing the analysis of the budget for 1977 and preparing the report for the Mayors and Selectmen and for the official vote to set the 1977 Budget."

"Hi Eleanor." I had just parked in front of her house in Jamaica Plain. I needed to finish the last analysis of one section of the report and I needed to review drafts of material provide me by Sue, Jose, and Eleanor earlier in the day.

"There's not much traffic out there at this hour," I said.

"And, it's a good idea not to be driving around at this hour," Eleanor responds.

"Every day, a new adventure," I said. "Besides, we can't be deterred."

"Come in." Eleanor said. "I have coffee, and some donuts. Sue has been here since about 9 P.M. She brought a second typewriter so that both she and I can type at the same time if need be. The entire document is in categories spread across my living room floor."

Sue looked up and came to the door. "Welcome. You know if they funded this office as well as they fund themselves, we'd have a half dozen people doing the charts and graphs and it would all be produced between 9 A.M. and 5 P.M. on a large conference room table, instead of between 9 A.M. and the following 9 A.M. on a living room floor.

"And look at you. It's 2 A.M. and you are just getting here."

"I know," I said. "but I also know from the phone conversations we've had every half-hour or so that you've been very busy finishing your pieces, as have I.

"How are you both doing?" I asked. "Can you make it for a couple more hours?"

"We have to have all the proofs done and everything assembled before 9 A.M.," Eleanor said.

"If I have the entire document on my desk by 9 A.M.— over 400 pages I'd estimate, I can make any minor corrections, assemble it and get it to the printer in time to make our deadline," said Sue.

"The people on the street and in the media who slam public servants so often have no idea about dedication," I said. "Sue, Eleanor, my heartfelt appreciation for your commitment to finish a job that you started. You are rare and wonderful people."

"We said we'd do it," said Sue. "It's not good to not finish what you start. Besides, I simply cannot abide turning in something that is incomplete and sloppy."

I hugged her.

Sue was the junior member of our team. Her job was to handle all the office management and secretarial tasks and to be thoughtful, accurate and detailed. She fit our requirements perfectly. This young, attractive, talkative woman was compulsive—the perfect trait for this job. Her past jobs had all been secretarial. She was smart and could do more than that, but no one ever expected anything of her. Consequently she was just delighted to take assignments that she knew mattered. She was delighted enough that she was a welcome part of our team even at this absurd hour. Fortunately, we only had one night like this one. However, the past two weeks have been long days with additional work at home as we systematically took each dark corner of the MBTA and put a spot light on it.

Eleanor had other reasons for wanting this project to be a success. She and her high-profile husband had recently divorced. Eleanor, very capable, super-organized, a thorough researcher and good analytically, was at last emerging from the shadows. She was a diminutive person who spoke very softly. She always held her own and had important things to say, but seldom had the opportunity. Her ex-husband was a fine man, although so caught-up in his own world and career that he may have taken her for granted. And his interests wandered. In taking this job, Eleanor found herself valued for what she could do. Part of her assignments, as we refined our examination of the MBTA's prior year budget and their proposals, was to compare MBTA costs with that of other comparable government bureaucracies. She spent many hours with the one or two really competent budget analysts from area cities. They highly respected her work and it was great to see her appreciated.

"Let's see what we have left to do." I said. "You both know the major objective here. This is the third year since the MBTA has needed to deal with the new management and with the Mayors and Selectmen from all 79 of our municipalities. I look at it as a turning point. To that end, the design for this budget for calendar year 1977 is more complete than the reports we prepared in our first two years. This 1977 budget report is also a complete reference on the MBTA. The purpose of writing it this way is to do something that no one else has done— maybe ever in the life of the Authority. The purpose is to have one central place where anyone to see the exact structural components within the Authority. People can see the manpower levels. That way, hopefully, those who want to make change can see what must be done. Those who have problems with MBTA performance can move past the general complaining to pinpointing the exact problem and the first step toward solving it."

"There's another thing I like about what we're doing this year," Eleanor said. "I like that they *say* that the Budget Analysis Office should provide for the concerns of the cities and towns that pay for the Authority. They *say* that such a great thing has been accomplished in making this office a part of the new law passed in 1973.

And, they are right in *saying* that. But, they didn't really want all that or they would have funded our office at a level that made it possible to really deliver. Therefore, we have no choice but to do this thorough report—mostly because they don't think we can do it."

Eleanor banged her coffee cup on the table to emphasize her point. Unusually emphatic for Eleanor.

"Right-on, Eleanor," said Sue, banging her cup. "Pass me another donut!"

"Pass me a donut, too," I say trying to bring us back to the job at hand. "The first item is to be sure we have everything we need to produce a quality document. I appreciate your sentiments and I certainly want to do what we have set forth to do, but it will all lose its value if it gets frosted with 'smug.' We need the document to be judged on its merit.

I turn to Sue.

"Sue, do you have the Advisory Board's Budget Committee recommendation as the first item?

This committee of seven, a sort of Advisory Board Executive Committee, is the people for whom I worked, and with whom I met monthly. At our last meeting, they had approved a transmittal that the highlighted key issues of concern and the dollars we were recommending the full Advisory Board approve.

I continued my directions to Sue. "Next, please put the Chairman's letter transmitting his request? And don't forget to put next the legal mandate for the MBTA Advisory Board of 79 municipalities to establish the final approved budget."

"Every year someone on our Board as well as reporters in the media get all confused about our role. That word 'advisory' is the problem."

I explained to Sue and Jose.

"When the original law was crafted creating a legislature to approve the MBTA budget, the MBTA legal office probably got some friendly legislator to slip the word 'advisory' into the name. From the MBTA's point of view, they knew that they wouldn't escape having a legislative body approve their budget submissions, but they found a way to sabotage it by confusing people about its role. It's a pity that neither the public nor the media nor some of our own members fully appreciate how mighty the pen is when one drafts legislation and ads a word here, or a comma there."

"I've got all that ready for the final packet," Sue said. "You're right about our name. I run into people all the time who don't understand what we do."

"Then we get into the body of the report. Thank you, Eleanor, for the pie charts and graphs. You've been doing a lot of drawing. I think it helps people compare things at a glance, more easily than with just text."

"Fortunately, I found some jar tops that are just the right size for drawing circles," Eleanor says. "Calculating the points on the graphs takes some time. I never thought I'd do this kind of math again. But it's fun." Eleanor must have prepared close to a hundred charts and graphs.

A sidebar to my colleagues on the train, I say "you sit here with your laptops and cell phones. Try to remember that the people who are in this story are engaged in dealing with this $240+ million operating budget and a capital budget of equal size 'before' personal computers, before power point or excel, before cell phones, before printers. The Authority had some leased space on main frame computers to tabulate their internal financial reports. While these were a step forward, they were quite primitive by today's standard, and they were managed by people who made no effort to go beyond tabulation to analysis. The Mayors and Selectman's staff had typewriters, carbon paper, had drawn graphs. Fortunately they did have the use of hand held calculators by the late 1970s."

I asked my staff as we finished organizing the final report, "Are we absolutely certain that for each department within the Authority we have the narrative breakdown that includes a) the department purpose, b) its organization and operation, c) its 1976 achievements, its 1977 outlook and objectives, d) the Chairman's exact budget request, e) the Advisory Board comments? This, of course, follows the Table of Organization for each Department."

"I think we have all those. Eleanor and I were double checking before you arrived." Sue noted.

"And, of course, wherever it's relevant, I assume that you have the data that shows manpower and salary trends, overtime trends, operating hour trends for vehicles, down time for vehicles, and all those many other specific pieces of data analysis that look like spaghetti when in a chart, but suddenly take on meaning when tied to a specific aspect of service delivery and when portrayed in a picture to accompany the words? Do you have the chart at the end that shows the formula indicating what percentage of the deficit each of our 79 communities must pay?"

"Yes, yes, yes. Don't worry so. I think we really have it ready to assemble," said Sue.

"Great. Let me help you with this last bit."

We worked together assembling the completed master document.

"Now, there's only one of these in the whole world, so, Sue, don't have a car accident and don't leave it out where your dog will pee on it between 4 A.M. and 9 A.M. Drive home slowly." Eleanor spoke for both of us as we watched Sue leave with the master budget report in her briefcase.

"Thank you both. You are beyond wonderful." I hug them and go to my car in hopes of a few hours of sleep before morning.

The 400+ page report goes off to the printer and then is mailed out to all 79 municipalities plus the MBTA Board of Directors and the Chairman, the Governor and other key officials. Major media are sent copies. The holidays come and go and it's the final date on which we can approve the 1977 budget. December 30, 1976. The Advisory Board meets.

The MBTA Chairman begins. "This is the third year since the new law restructuring the MBTA passed. We've not reached our objectives yet for turning the MBTA into a system with increased ridership, maximum productivity and a reasonable budget, but we're beginning to make some serious progress toward those objectives. We have tightened the budget belt to the point where the departments now know that there will be no supplemental budgets. The historic pattern of coming back for more money nearly once a month was shameful. We've added discipline to our capital budget to more sharply focus on the fact that new construction must relate to our regional transportation goals. There's more discipline in setting service standards that respond to public interests.

"We have made some internal savings. One in particular is the elimination of the 'guard' jobs, a point of contention for many years, since these employees who ride between rail cars have no safety assignments. They merely watch the automatic doors open and shut—a job controlled by the train operator. We've cut the number of spare buses to a more industry-acceptable level and we've eliminated some of the private vehicles that are not used for transit service. Further efficiencies must combine with plant and fleet upgrades and the new fare collection system. In short, we are making improvements to the operations of this corporation in every department—from the contracts with the unions to the investment policies, to benefit options, to repair and operational systems. I'm pleased with our progress to date. I'm especially pleased with the number of employees who have come on board committed to help make the new MBTA one in which they can be proud to work. I wish it could all be accomplished yesterday. But we are well on our way."

"Thank you Mr. Chairman," says the MBTA Advisory Board Chair. "Now, let's hear from our Director of Budget Analysis."

"This is also our third year operating under the new law," I said. By shining some light into all the corners of this large bureaucracy, we're both keeping the pressure on the MBTA, letting them know that the elected officials who must put the deficit on their property tax bills are watching and can embarrass them if they screw up.

"This kind of scrutiny is also having another benefit in that a number of forgotten bureaucrats who once cared but never were heard are now beginning to think that someone might even listen to their ideas, to what they know better than anyone who comes in without direct experience. As a result, internal savings are being found and increased productivity is beginning to happen.

"We have reduced budget increases in these three years, and that has prevented the kind of deficit increases that otherwise would have been on automatic pilot. We have pressured for tighter oversight of the relationship between the operating and capital budget because the capital budget can either increase or stabilize, maybe decrease, some operating costs. We've made some real cuts in expenditures. However, this is not a ship to be turned around with the snap of one's fingers. I think it will take another three years to really see significant results, simply because so much of what must be done requires implementing new procedures, using updated equipment, negotiating new contracts for benefits or for unions, and even changing existing laws.

"I am gratified about the number of phone calls I have received from within the Authority asking for a copy of our 1977 Budget Report and Complete Reference on the MBTA. [2] To have persons who supervise work areas within the MBTA, or who work in the media, or who are public officials in Eastern Massachusetts want to understand why a given problem exists and what is needed to solve it can only help move this process forward. It's quite astonishing that prior to this change of law individual department heads had no idea how they fit within the context of the whole agency, and no idea of where they might turn to solve a problem or test a new idea or find a new efficiency."

"I'd say to you that providing coherent quantifiable data analysis may be our major accomplishment to date in addition to curbing supplemental budgets and preventing expected deficit escalation. Our research project of 1976, the analysis of funding options, must receive follow-up attention from the MBTA itself and the Governor's Office. Aside from the wide range of taxing options, there are, in my opinion, ways to develop more private:public partnerships that can be financially successful and the MBTA has greatly underutilized its extensive real estate holdings. [3]

"We're not there yet; but we are moving toward our objectives at a deliberate speed."

Counterpoint Three

Government Change-Making Requires More Than Reorganizing

"Why don't they have a working TV in here?" Paul asked anyone who might answer him. No one listening would have the answer. It's still just the five of us in the AMTRAK Club Car.

Paul's had enough coffee. He can't sleep. The train is still clickety-clacking its way across the country and the ride seems likely never to end. The story-telling is O.K., but it wouldn't be his first choice for entertainment. An exciting game on ESPN would be better.

"Hey, look at it this way, Paul," says Ted, "you'd never hear about this stuff if we hadn't had to take this train. The plane would have landed by now and we'd be off to wherever we were headed."

"Yeah," said John. "I'd be having a nightcap and I'd go to bed in a comfortable hotel room."

"But things didn't turn out that way, so let's talk," I said. "What did you think of the effort to bring some changes to a huge public transportation bureaucracy?" I asked.

"Sure took me inside the bowels of a big government bureaucracy," said Paul.

"Who cares?" said John. "Let's just continue this story-telling until we get off this damn train. Nothing else to do."

"Ordinarily, I wouldn't care about your story," said Paul. "And I certainly won't remember much of what you said about putting together the budget. But I'll remember what the toll collector puts up with not being able to change a light bulb. And I'll remember what goes on in the repair shop where everyone's job is to be boss and no one's job is to repair the vehicles."

Paul says, "the story makes a new point for me. It's not just one huge entity that's ripping off my tax dollars; it's the lots and lots of little operations within the huge entity. If you can't pay attention to the detail, you can't fix the problem. You gotta know who within each bureaucracy is trying to get it right, who's screwing up, and you gotta know who can't get it right because the laws, regulations and work rules need to be changed.

"Thing is," Paul continues, "I don't think that, as a taxpayer, I should need to know all those details. I should just expect it to be fixed so I get my money's worth. I gotta trust that the people in charge are paying attention to all this detail, but I don't know if they are."

"But if you and I don't hear the details, how can the spotlight shine in the right place? How can there be enough pressure so that anything really gets fixed?" asks Richard.

"Maybe you're right," says Paul. "It usually does take the squeaky wheel to get some grease where it's needed.

"So let the media shine the light on what's wrong."

"Now, wait a minute," says Ted. "My News Director wouldn't cover this stuff—not beyond a blurb announcing that the law changed and there's new leadership."

Ted stands up and walks to one end of the car. He turns back, "If he did cover it, I'd probably have him fired. We can't keep our ratings up enough to get good priced ads by covering this kind of news. You'd put the viewers to sleep."

"And that's not just us," Ted continues. "No one would cover these details. Neither would you find it in blogs or on twitter or Face Book—not unless some arcane group of transit buffs who work within the bureaucracy have nothing better to do than bitch to each other late at night."

Paul also paces to the end of the car and back. He's had his say. For one who just cares about the tax bill, he's actually taken a slightly new look at how to get to his goal—less cost. Now, he'll just pace and listen.

"Just think of it," Ted says. "The evening news comes on. A drum roll and flashing graphic say 'breaking news' and the reporter says 'today a toll collector in the subway made the wrong change because the light bulb over his toll booth was out. Give me a break."

Ted continues. "People don't want that stuff. They want a dead body, or a big scandal where some public official has absconded with millions, or at least a train wreck with ambulances. People don't want a lecture on how to fix government."

"Are you telling me that people just want good service, low taxes and no information on where good work is done or where the problems are." Richard chimes in.

"Sure," Ted answers. That's all that counts."

"I think that's what you want us to think," says Richard. "Your job is easier that way. But how can we ever solve problems if we can't understand what's wrong and what's needed to find solutions? And how can the good people who do their jobs working in the bureaucracy get anything but debilitated if all they ever get is a massive 'you're rotten' and no one ever hears their problems or praises them when they get it right?"

"I don't understand what the big deal is," says John. "Why didn't the Governor and the Legislature just leave the transportation system alone? Sure the cities were complaining about high taxes. But so what? The trains weren't getting derailed. Just tell the public that costs are up everywhere and it can't be helped. Tell them that, if they keep complaining, that you'll cut their service."

John, sounding like the long time entrepreneur and business executive that he is, continues. "Stability is a good thing. Let sleeping dogs lie. A bureaucracy with 6,000 people has been running for decades and the guys in charge know how to keep things running. What's the point in disrupting everything? What's the point in making more work? All these changes in law and management did is to make more work. And that could cost more money, not less."

Now Richard was getting angry. "John, you just don't get it. It's all about you and your buddies who run things and make the money; you don't care about whether people get the services they pay for. I think you don't care because those people are invisible to you unless they somehow disrupt your Swiss-watch operation. Cut some ribbons. Hold some meetings. Give employees a watch when they retire. Smile at the photo ops. Fit in a few banquets and maybe a junket or two to meet colleagues from elsewhere. Just don't upset the life-style and the money flow."

John replied. "The trains keep running. What more do you want?"

"John, we're modern now." Richard was determined to make his point to John. "We can do things we couldn't do fifty years ago. Why use an abacus when you can use a computer? Why run transportation services from where people used to live to where they used to go when you could keep the paying public happier and—I might add—bring in more revenue by responding to today's needs and interests? It might even be better for you."

Richard continues. "Aside from times changing, there is such a thing as decent management, John. You know very well that if you need to cut costs, you can refinance debt, cut overtime, consolidate operations to prevent duplication, explore new revenue options. You can do a zillion things before you need to cut service. You're just tossing out excuses to keep the media and the taxpayers off your back. You just want to rake in the income with the least possible amount of work."

"You're not going to get more revenue from more riders until you get more PR," says Ted. "I don't know how you can do something spectacular enough to get that PR just now. What could you possibly offer that would send crowds to mass transit the way they flock to a carnival or a sports event?"

Ted, the media executive, tries to be helpful by putting on his management hat. "It's not my job to think about how you get to the point of being spectacular. But, I'd guess that one has to hope that 'spectacular' can come out of the changes described in the story."

Ted continues. "For example, as a manager in the private sector, I've made management changes to solve some real problems. It's harder in the public sector because the power isn't concentrated in one CEO. You need to deal with laws and different branches of government, checks and balances, and you need to deal with elections and public opinion. And you need to deal with all the personalities and self-interests that influence whether or not someone will support the change you suggest, and a lot of that garbage has nothing what-so-ever to do with the substance of the issue at hand. It has to do with politics and whim. If, in this case, the law change actually tightens up accountability with the new Executive reporting to the Governor, that could be good. If increasing the resources for the Legislative branch by giving the mayors and selectmen an office with skilled staff to monitor the budget, that could be good—if it's not setting up better armed warfare between Executive and Legislative."

Ted smiles. "Actually, it was clever to follow-up the law change with a strategic plan that has the new budget analyst for the Mayors and Selectmen be the person who first does the investigation of the system first, before the new Chairman arrives, and then be the person to brief the Chairman before he begins his job. That process accomplished several things. It let the staffer for the Advisory Board make the case on the status of the system and what improvements are needed. It makes it in the interest of the Chairman to hear what the Advisory Board has to say. It gives credibility to the Advisory Board work by incorporating these briefing documents into management's own assessment. Finally, when the executive branch of the MBTA and legislative branch need to assume their required opposition roles at budget time, this prior briefing will result in there having been enough collaboration between the two offices for both to understand their common goal is greater than simply having budget stand-offs. They will both have a self-interest of resolving budget disputes within a context that leads to overall improvement of service delivery and cost-effectiveness."

"Clever." Ted commented as he thought about his own management strategies within his media company. "But none of that is PR. Real 'reform' will need a minimum of three years before they can get things lined up enough to do anything that might thrill the public, and get the media coverage that amplifies how thrilled the public is," Ted comments.

"Do I have to wait that long to see my taxes go down?" Paul asked. "We normal people don't like to wait that long.

If someone says 'elect us and we'll bring change,' we expect the change—six weeks max. I do admit that this story has me appreciating that it's not always possible to make our system of laws and checks-and-balances work in six weeks. But I'd never have paid attention to this if I hadn't been captive audience on this train. No one else pays attention. So, how're you gonna get people to be patient?"

"At the end of the day, you still need to keep the trains running. That matters more than new-fangled ideas. To do that, you just need to know that you have the revenue source to keep running. The budget doesn't matter much because tax revenue is guaranteed by law." John concludes. He slumps in his train seat and gets ready for a snooze.

"Now, that's a scary thought!" Paul chimes in. "I wonder how many public officials just keep taxing us because they can? How many stash away, or spend away, our hard earned dollars just because they can? Does nobody keep the pressure on to manage money wisely? In this story we just heard, the Governor and those who passed the new law will feel some public pressure to make sure that the results bring promised savings. But the public can't pay attention for several years. Only the real transit advocates will do that. And if the media doesn't cover what's happening, eventually things will get so bad again that the public just gets fed-up and decide that the great new plan didn't work either."

"Here's a totally different story," I say. "You're right that unless the people play their role—keep insisting that they get good service at reasonable costs, things will erode. That's a whole problem of its own—how to have people know that they are part of the problem if they aren't active enough to be part of the solution. But, please don't get so lost in the 'big picture' that you forget to notice that it is in the 'little pictures' that scores of people are making changes in public policy— nickel and dime democracy. Individuals in this story began to see that it is in their self-interest to help make things operate better. And so, step-by-step, things began to operate better. Maybe that's the only way democracy ever builds-up a credible enough performance record to be viable with the public. Maybe that's the strategic plan that makes 'reorganization' of a huge bureaucracy actually work."

The Third Story—FEMA Plan to Evacuate in Nuclear Attack

Run! First Responders Will Protect You From a Nuclear Attack!

CIVIC EDUCATION, A NEWSLETTER, AND NETWORKING
AMONG PROFESSIONALS IN FIELD

"Can you believe what the federal government is spending tax dollars on now?" Alex reconvenes the group at the conference.

It's October, 1981. The huge maple trees surrounding us must have been standing when the Dutch first settled this area along the Hudson River just north of New York City. The day is gorgeous—crisp fall air, totally blue sky. The lawn runs slightly downhill until it reaches into the deeper blue river. It's a treat to walk through the leaves that have just started to fall, large red maple leaves, brown oak leaves, yellows from the elm trees. How fortunate can we be, finding ourselves spending a weekend at this elegant estate!

"Did you get your coffee?" Josie asks Pam. Newell, Phil, Pam and Randy seem reluctant to end their conversation and sit down again. I sit next to Josie.

"Something is out-of-order," George notes. "Look at this wonderful group of people, this idyllic environment and this spectacular day. And instead of spending our Saturday going for walks in the woods, we're gathered in here to discuss shifts in U.S. foreign policy that can threaten the American homeland with increased risk of nuclear war. Sick! Don't you think?"

George always had a skill for slicing through any situation with perceptive comments. And again, he's right.

"I'm glad we are meeting to discuss this issue," says Margaret, a scientist who was part of the movement to stop atmospheric nuclear tests in the early 1960s, a generation ago. "Defending America is our common agenda here. There's more to defending America than simply building and testing and counting nuclear arsenals, although you might not remember that if you spend all your time in the scientific community as I do. Defending America is the public's common agenda too. There's more to defending it than trusting that the scientific community and the government will think and act broadly enough to protect the public. You could easily not remember that point if you immersed yourself in the usual activities of raking leaves, shopping, fixing the kids' meals and thinking about your particular job or interests. Frankly, if the government and the scientists fuck up, the public pays the price."

Margaret continues, "It was the public who finally convinced the political and bureaucratic leadership to change public policy in the 1960s. We saved a lot of kids from drinking radiated milk when we finally succeeded in securing the Atmospheric Test Ban Treaty, and it hasn't hurt the defense effort one bit for them to test underground rather than spread radioactive materials wherever the wind is blowing. A lot of people's lives are better because, in that case, a pesky group of change-makers made their case and were persistent in arguing and following through on every detail."

I say to my club car colleagues, "it's been over twenty years since this story happened, and the irony is that now, again, in this new era called a 'War on Terrorism' we have nuclear weapons small enough to fit in a briefcase. Maybe we should once again revisit the matter of protecting our civilian population."

This elegant room with its floor-to-ceiling windows is full of about 50 people attending today's conference. We had gathered to evaluate the status and strategy for the rapidly growing "Call to Halt the Nuclear Arms Race"—The *Freeze* movement.

We were an odd assortment of academics, scientists, Quaker peace activists, a few people with political involvements and those concerned about the consequences of ignoring this issue. Yes, there are some young typical 'activists,' but this group has more older people than is often the case when people come together to advocate change. That's probably because those who learned about the problem of unsecured radioactive materials at the time of the 1960s efforts to win the Atmospheric Test Ban. After the Ban was signed, the press and the people went home. Everything had been fixed, hadn't it? Now, twenty years later, people were beginning to gather again to take note of the huge expansion of nuclear proliferation that has happened globally in the past twenty years. This re-awakened interest is a direct response to President Reagan's comment about 'firing a warning shot' across the bow for the Soviet Union to see how powerful our weapons are. As new groups gather and are educated by the scientific community about our current strategic weapon national defense, they become increasingly appalled about whether or not enough safeguards are in place to prevent accidental use of these weapons and to protect the very people who should be protected by this deterrent force.

George Sommaripa is here. He's Harvard trained in law and history with an early career interest as a Bible scholar. He focuses mostly on politics and writing about preventing use of nuclear weapons. He is the co-author of *The Price of Defense*. Pam Solo is also here. She had been a Roman Catholic nun committed to peace work. Newell Mack came. He had grown up at Los Alamos where his dad had been the head of photography for the Manhattan Project; he is valued for his strategic thinking and ability to connect the abstract and the practical. And he is zealously committed to protecting future generations from the dragon he saw unleashed in the first Atomic Bomb tested where he grew up. Part of the Harvard community, too, Newell seeks to link excellence in research with those whose job it is to implement safeguards. Josie Murray is here. She's a pediatrician by training, daughter of Harvard's psychology professor Dr. Henry A. Murray, and a philanthropist. Randy Forsberg is an MIT researcher focusing on nuclear arms control, a co-author of *The Price of Defense,* and a founder of the Nuclear Freeze Movement. Randy Kehler is here. He's a former teacher and founder of Traprock Peace Center. He's had special interest in U.S. Senator Mark Hatfield's (R-Oregon) amendment to SALT II concerning curbing expansion of nuclear arsenals. I'd been invited because, at the time, I was Deputy Executive Director of the Union of Concerned Scientists, a nationwide non-profit association concerned about responsible use of nuclear weapons materials.

"So, do you want to hear how the feds are spending our tax dollars now?" Alex asks again. "Here's the latest.

"Hot off the press in December 1980, FEMA, the Federal Emergency Management Agency has a new tool for disaster management. Picture this. You're driving down the highway when you hear an air raid siren. Instantly you stop your car, by the side of the road, if possible. You jump out. You pull a shovel out of your trunk along with the FEMA directions for creating a nuclear attack shelter for yourself and anyone with you."

"What do they mean by 'shelter?'" Someone asks.

"Here it is. Allow me to describe this 'shelter.'" Alex comments as he pulls out the press release from FEMA. "FEMA sent out across the nation camera-ready newspaper columns in

December 1980. I guess they wanted to be certain that they had done their best to educate the public—in case anyone suggests that they aren't doing their job." He passed around the press release.

"Oh, look at this. Here's what you do after you park your car," said the person closest to Alex. "You dig a hole two feet deep under your car. The diagram in their press release even shows where you can put a dirt step to get in and out."

"But you need to plan carefully," said another person also looking at the press release. "See, here it says that the first thing you do is to remove all seats from the car if possible. Cover the floor and trunk with plastic and one foot of earth on top of floor and trunk. I guess that gives you a place to put some of the dirt and also add more protection, plus—and here's the bonus—you get to use the car seats in your new home, the hole in the ground."

"Most important, don't forget the tarp," says another person looking at the press release and laughing. It says, explicitly, that you 'string a plastic tarp behind and in front of car.'"

"I guess that's in case there's a gentle rain that accompanies the fire storm and the hurricane force winds accompanying the blast," comments another person.

"Hey, FEMA means well. They have calculated how long it will take to create your shelter—the same way the IRS calculates the time it should take you to do your annual tax return. They say that two people working eight hours can get this done."

By now, everyone is roaring hilariously. It's all so absurd.

"What if my granny is driving alone? Maybe I just pack a shovel, a tarp and a sandwich for her," a tall fellow in the back of the room offered.

Similar cracks followed. FEMA had managed to do what most government agencies never are able to do and created a comedy show complete with a script and accompanying pictures. Prior to receiving these press releases, most people thought of FEMA as the agency that helped in emergency recovery from floods, hurricanes, tornados and similar disasters. Only people involved with the details of the nuclear arms race ever thought much about a civil defense from nuclear war. It had been a good forty years since the first Atomic Bomb was used and the issue of civilian defense hadn't arisen as an item of public discourse. Now, FEMA was being pro-active.

Right after World War II, when America was engaged in atmospheric testing, civil defense "Shelter" signs were tacked on buildings to indicate Fallout Shelters where, allegedly, the public would go to be safe from radiation. The concept had some validity in the late 1940s, but then technology changed greatly. K-12 schools across the nation set aside times for fire drills and "duck and cover" exercises. In a "duck and cover drill" the teacher would command all the students to crawl under their desks so they would be safe from an atomic blast. This exercise probably never had validity whatsoever. In the same era, people built "Bomb Shelters" on their property—underground shelters or space in their cellars where cots, candles and canned foods would keep the family safe from atomic blasts. That era lost news appeal when the Atmospheric Test Ban Treaty was signed in 1963 and fewer and fewer people have built bomb shelters over the last twenty years.

In 1980 the issue revived. This was probably due to the new administration in Washington supporting weapon modernization programs. There is a general sense that "duck and cover" is a concept best left behind. It served the past generation as a satire on how to find safety. The new policy emerging from FEMA in the 1980s is focused on evacuation—moving large city populations to small rural communities. The assumption is that the large city is the target for nuclear attack, not its population.

"For FEMA to suggest that it's possible to implement plans for surviving today's strategic nuclear explosions is so cruel. It only validates the level of ignorance. A nuclear attack is not a tornado scaled up one notch. Let me read you something." Randy Forsberg opened the book she'd brought, *Effects of Nuclear War*, published by the U.S. Office of Technology Assessment in 1979:

"Today's strategic nuclear weapons, as you all know, are much different from the first Atomic bomb used in Hiroshima—and look what that one small bomb did to Hiroshima.

A one megaton burst in area with uniform fifteen miles-per-hour wind speed provides the following accumulated dose of radiation over seven days if a person has no shielding:

3000 Rems		35 mi downwind
900	Rems	90 mi downwind
300	Rems	160 mi downwind
90	Rems	250 mi downwind

- If you are outside and only have your clothes to protect you, the radiation dose is lethal at 700-800 Rem.

- If you are in a frame house you'll receive some 300 Rem of radiation and have 50% chance to die.

- If you are in a basement, you'll receive a 100 Rem dose, and need treatment for radiation sickness. [1]

Randy continued, "the government issued health standards for radiation exposure limit nuclear workers to 0.5 Rem whole body dose per year and for typical persons a cap of 80 Millirem (x-rays, for example) per year. Natural background radiation exposure is between 80-190 Millirem per year depending on where a person is." Radiation accidents come from nuclear reactors, terrorist bombs as well as from war

Randy concluded, "wouldn't you think that one office of the federal government could talk with another office? Wouldn't you think that those guys at FEMA would at least find out what kind of civil defense hazard a strategic nuclear weapon explosion caused before they told all their offices across the U.S.A. that they know how to protect people?"

I turn back to those with whom I sit in the train car. "As you can see, this is a whole different situation from the last story I told you. These people do make change by getting one federal agency to pay attention to how it spends its money. But listen to the rest of the story. They do this in a very different way than did the people in the City of Somerville story, or the people in the State of Massachusetts transportation agency. They needed to be absolutely certain that nothing they did either 'in fact' or 'in perception' could divide people over the important objective of the best possible national defense for America. Here's what they did."

"By this time," I recounted, "the people attending the conference were settling down and were ready for the next speakers. Many of the people already knew what Randy was talking about, although it was useful for her to read the documents because some new persons were in attendance. Josie and I had been having a side conversation."

"Josie, Dr. Murray, is a wiry small-framed neatly dressed older woman," I tell my club car companions. "She's quick to understand and very smart. She knew everyone and everyone knew her. She'd grown up in the Harvard-Radcliffe community and had been very active in the scientific and peace groups concerned about reining-in potential disaster from nuclear weapons. That may have resulted, in part, from her experience during World War II working with the OSS, the U.S. government's Office of Strategic Services. When she finished medical school she worked in one of the nation's finest institutions serving children's physical and mental health. Her passions, aside from working to solve public health problems such as the nuclear safety matter, were classical music and her working farm north of Boston." She stated her interest in the discussion:

"I'm glad there's beginning to be a collection of individuals who realize how badly FEMA is doing its job, for so long people just laughed or dismissed them as irrelevant. Their errors could have serious consequences in addition to the waste of tax dollars."

I elaborated on my interest. "Most of my experience is city government and state government. Nonetheless, at any level of government or in any private corporation you would think that those in charge would not launch a huge public campaign until they were sure they had their facts right. Government people have to hear that from their constituents and from other government people, not from lofty scientists or people perceived as fuzzy-headed peace advocates.

140

"FEMA will come out of this looking foolish. A lot of First Responders who run Civil Defense, Fire and Police Departments across the U.S.A. will be asked to do the impossible and end up being blamed when things go wrong." I note. "It's a huge waste of taxpayer dollars. And then there's the idea that it sends out a suggestion that nuclear war is O.K and survivable. There goes the deterrent policy that it is unthinkable for anyone to use these weapons."

Josie agrees, and adds some of her own thoughts. "Randy didn't even talk about all the impacts of the explosion of a strategic weapon. For example, there'd likely be little, if any warning, of such an explosion and the 'war' or attack could begin and end in less than an hour. How does that set with those on the highway trying to dig the hole under their car in eight hours? I'm in my late 60s now and it would be a funny picture indeed to see me try to dig a hold under my car." She chuckles.

"I certainly couldn't get the car seats out. Let me analyze a child's illness in my medical office and I have some chance of doing that correctly, but I wouldn't know where to begin to remove car seats. And then—dig a hole? Well, I'd have to hope that I wasn't on asphalt. And if it's a dirt road, I hope the ground is soft. Don't know that I keep a shovel in my car. I really don't pay much attention to that sort of thing. What would happen if I called AAA? Quite aside from the timing problem, and the real possibility of a driver being able to dig the hole FEMA wants, there are other things FEMA has overlooked. For example, a person quite some distance from the actual blast could be instantly blinded by the intensity of the fire ball. You'd think, even if they don't check facts, that someone who works for FEMA might remember the photos from Hiroshima. And today's bombs are so much more powerful. The blast intensity would destroy everything within thirty miles, maybe more. People could have second degree burns or worse and considerable destruction as far as 250 square miles from the detonation site."

"I know, Josie," I add. "Did you see Kevin Lewis's article in *Scientific American*? He talked about how the firestorm at Hiroshima lasted six hours totally destroying 4.4 square miles of city. He pointed out that the weapons used today would be bigger than the Hiroshima 15 kiloton one by two or three orders of magnitude. And he compared that event almost forty years ago with what might happen in an American city today. He discussed how American cities are far more developed with gasoline and heating oil everywhere available to fuel the fires." [2]

Josie chimes in again. "What I love about the FEMA plan is the plastic tarps. Do they really think that when the fire storm sucks the oxygen out of the shelters, the plastic on the tarps won't melt? Then, of course, FEMA's press release stops before the next question is raised. If radiation is lethal over as much as 600 square miles and food, water, and air can be contaminated from radiation over an area of 4,000 square miles, what do those of us under our cars do on the day after?"

Josie stopped and reached into her purse. "Here's $10. Use it to start a newsletter informing the public about the absurdity of what's being proposed to defend our civilian population. I'll help you with it."

That single act was the beginning of a new idea that would be turned into a reality—making sure that no one forgot the real protection of the population that we say we plan to protect as the ultimate objective of the nuclear arms race. The objective would be no different than was the objective of those who ultimately secured an atmospheric test ban treaty—remember to protect the home front. Not only would people across the nation think seriously about what First Responders could and could not do; even Washington D.C. policy makers would be pushed to change their policy. Josie was making change—the nickel and dime kind that resulted in sustained change greater than any emerging from a nine second soundbite in the media.

Josie and I turned our attention back to the conference agenda.

Randy Forsberg led the discussion involving some of the scientists in the room about the recently developed "Call to Halt the Nuclear Arms Race" (*The Freeze)* as a strategy that could enable people to understand that we already have far more than sufficient nuclear weapons to destroy the Soviet Union many times over and vice-versa. It would be a waste of money and foolish to continue to escalate the arms race. The objective of *The Freeze* strategy was not to disarm. It was not to abandon nuclear arsenals. It was simply to say, let's *Freeze* where we are. Many scientists who knew the warhead and missile data and who understood the concept of MAD–mutual assured destruction–as a deterrent to war, liked the *Freeze* strategy because it was a feasible way to curb the start of a whole new arms race that might well come with the currently discussed arsenal modernization plans.

Randy Forsberg was very efficient, detailed, accurate and in charge. She was young—mid-thirties maybe, and she had to have the talents noted above to have a seat at the table with the male MIT scientists. Aside from earning their respect scientifically, she had one quality that some of the scientists did not have. She could translate the technical concerns into English so normal people could understand them.

"I know you didn't sanction our putting the *Freeze* on ballots in western Massachusetts towns last fall," said a tall young man in the back of the room. "We just did it. But, I think the results tell a lot. Thirty of thirty-three of the towns that Ronald Reagan won in November, 1980, voted in favor of the call to *Freeze* the nuclear arms race. That means that people are concerned about the risks we pose for ourselves and the costs we incur for nuclear weapons, even though they support the Reagan-Bush call for a military build-up.

"You've got to get used to the fact that if this is a 'movement' and not an 'organization'," he concluded "you won't be able to approve or disapprove every action everyone takes. The *Freeze* must become an enormous social movement embraced by people all across the nation, supported by every possible group of individuals doing what makes sense to them and their friends in their town. We're a big nation. We have a lot of differing views."

"Yes," Randy Kehler answered. "But we must be very sure that grass-roots citizens understand how this issue effects them. We can't have people be as ill-informed as those in the FEMA office or we will never succeed."

Randy was careful. He was right to be careful; in the public arena when the media amplify any thing at any time, one must have a credible enough base of support to survive whatever attacks may come.

The decision had been made to establish a national office for the *Freeze* in St. Louis—an easy central point for involvement from everywhere in the nation. Randy Kehler was to be the Executive Director.

The conference continued. The conversations went on until it was time to head back home. The little side-bar between Josie and me was to be quite independent of the *Freeze* as an organization. Our interests may have overlapped, but our specific agendas were different and our constituencies were very different.

Matthew, from central Massachusetts, was in Cambridge the following week. We told him about Josie's idea to create a national newsletter about how people were dealing with FEMA's plan to have big cities evacuate to small towns to be safe from nuclear war, and about the camera-ready press releases coming to communities from FEMA's Washington, D.C., office.

"Great," said Matthew. "People need to know what's going on—especially since we, the taxpayer, are paying. You know, where I live in Greenfield, MA, is well over an hour's drive from Cambridge, and some of the trip is on two-lane or three-lane roads. You're telling me that all 100,000 of you from Cambridge are coming to Greenfield to be safe from nuclear war?"

"Yes. Don't you want us to come?" Mark was eager to fill him in. "It will be O.K. because they have it figured out. Want to hear how?"

"Sure," said Matthew grinning, assuming Mark's comment was tongue-in-cheek.

"If your car has an even number at the end of the license plate, you come on an even numbered day of the month. If your license plate ends with an odd number, you come the next day. Don't you think that helps?"

"Oh, my God! You have to be kidding. A bunch of kids up in a bar all night couldn't think of something this crazy," Matthew said.

"Well," Mark says, trying not to laugh. "It will really work out because the local First Responders will be assigned to checking license plates at every road out of town. That way traffic will be orderly and those guys won't get distracted trying to collect their children from school and get their families on the road to your town."

"You have a point," Matthew says continuing the parody. "And I suppose it won't all really matter since any nuclear attack will begin and end in an hour's time. That'll bring a quick end to the traffic jam and make life easier at the local supermarket in Greenfield."

"Josie called me earlier today," I said. "She found a way to have the Cambridge Civil Defense Director make a presentation to the City Council next week. He'll ask permission to send a letter to the federal government saying Cambridge refuses to participate in such cruel illusion. She said that the word about this is spreading quickly among the community of 'grey beards' who fought for an end to atmospheric testing twenty years ago. Add those folks to the MIT and Harvard scientific communities and there are a lot of influential people who can go to City Council."

The week passed until the City Council meeting and, as tends to happen in Cambridge, each passing day new ideas were generated about how best to handle this item on the Council agenda. Meanwhile, some of the Council Members were getting telephone calls from local citizens telling them about the public safety disaster that they'd have if a nuclear detonation happened in Cambridge.

Some Council Members were very interested in the issues of the day and were part of or worked closely with the academic communities. Other members of the Council, the ones who were sick of allegedly elitist academics, the ones who were 'the townies' in the 'town:gown' political community, were especially angry. They weren't going to let the feds tell Cambridge how to spend tax dollars. And they certainly weren't going to adopt a policy that put First Responders in the position of being blamed when a plan didn't work. They didn't know too much about nuclear weapons, but they did know that on a Friday afternoon the traffic was bumper-to-bumper with no one able to get out of town. And that traffic jam didn't even include all the people you'd have in a mandatory evacuation. It was a 'no-brainer.'

The night of the Council Meeting, City Hall was full.

The Mayor announced the FEMA agenda item. The Civil Defense Director spoke about the logistical impossibility of evacuating the city. Elaine Kistiakowsky, active in Cambridge politics, brought her husband, retired Harvard Professor George Kistiakowsky. George had been the Director of the Implosion Division at the Los Alamos Manhattan Project laboratories. George spoke about what would actually happen if a strategic nuclear weapon were intentionally or accidentally detonated. Paul Walker and George Sommaripa had materials from their book, *The Price of Defense.* A motion to reject the FEMA plan was easily passed.

But, before the Council meeting was over, more happened.

Someone said, "Every time I enter the main Post Office in Central Square I walk past that rusted metal black and yellow sign telling me that the Post Office is a Fallout Shelter."

Another commented, "I'd like to see how many of us would be safe in that large lobby. For heavens sake, the entire room is surrounded by gigantic windows."

One of the researchers in the audience said he wanted to provide for the record a copy of "Civil Defense Circular 73-7: Redirection of National Shelter Program." The page he turned over to the Council stated that "the term 'best available shelter' should not be misinterpreted. It's not necessarily 'safe shelter' shelter that is guaranteed to save persons or keep them safe in a disaster. Rather it is the safest area in each building that has been rated."

"That's doubletalk," said Sandra Graham, a very smart outspoken City Council Member. I get so sick of people hiding behind their titles and nobody raises an eyebrow while they tell you this stuff that they have to know makes no sense—just to cover their asses. How's a normal person, say a mother and her kids, maybe a family from the black community near the Central Square Post Office, supposed to know whether or not she's taking good care of her kids when she takes them to the Fallout Shelter here? Don't you think most intelligent persons would think that if the government said 'here's a shelter' under the auspices of the people keeping the people safe, that the shelter would indeed keep the people safe? We need to get rid of these Fallout Shelter signs!"

Another Member of City Council agreed with Graham. Council voted to get rid of the signs.

Council then turned to the topic of educating the public about the policy decisions that were made in D.C. that affected those of us who live in Cambridge. They decided to educate the Cambridge community on the hazards of nuclear war by publishing a booklet. They appropriated the money to do so and hired a young local lawyer, Larry Beeferman, to write the manuscript. The finished booklet was mailed at city expense to every household on the city's list.

Josie and I had lunch shortly after all this happened.

"I'm reeling," said Josie. "So much has happened so quickly. You know the public may not be informed on the details of issues. They may not know how to solve a problem or whose job it is to solve it. But the public is a quick study when something is wrong. They know enough to know that FEMA should stick to managing hurricane and earthquake relief and stay away from Nuclear War protection. Hopefully, they can manage those disasters better than this kind of disaster."

"I'm getting similar responses when talking with people about the newsletter we discussed." I say. "People think it's a great way to make it possible for First Responders to exchange information with each other. Because I've had several local government jobs, I know some of the local First Responders and they'll tell me what they think. The newsletter must have only information useful to them in their jobs. No peace community touchy-feely pie-in-the-sky stuff. No political advocacy. It's hard enough for busy people to deal with new ideas that come from outside the regular bureaucracy channels. I think we make it harder if our message gets entangled with larger issues of a Nuclear *Freeze* or with anyone's bias for or against any political candidate."

I pushed my point.

"This whole project can go in a waste basket as another 'feel good' advocacy project by people who want to tell others how to do something. We mustn't let that happen. The newsletter content must be mostly First Responders from one place telling their story to First Responders at another location. The folks who read the newsletter are in charge of protecting the public. They're smart. They can look at the facts surrounding a nuclear detonation and decide for themselves whether or not they think they can make FEMA's plan work. Let's just get out of the way and let them figure it out."

"Let's do it," said Josie. "We'll work together on it."

The newsletter was to be principally financed by subscription, and—amazingly–it worked. People were really eager to read what their colleagues had to say. And they were happy to make connections with professionals faced with the same obstacles in places far removed from their own communities.

A year-and-a-half passed. In early 1984 several of us were at Josie's farm in Topsfield for a party

"While we're all here, let's talk for a minute about what's happened since the nuclear civil defense awareness national newsletter started," I said to Matthew and to Josie. Newell was there too.

"You know," Josie said, 'if this were a peace movement activity or a civil rights event, you'd measure what happens by how many people show up for the events you sponsor. I'm not sure we can size this up that way."

Newell stood leaning against the wall puffing on his pipe. His huge frame was always imposing. His full beard tended to mask some of the expressions he'd have on his face. Newell, the Harvard professor-type, was at Harvard and among those weighing important matters, but was never the professor because he couldn't abide the bureaucracy, the trivia, the university politics. Always a bit rumpled, Newell usually looked like he had grabbed the clothes thrown on the floor the night before and, if the morning had carried him away before he got to comb his hair—well, so what. People should know what's important! All this appearance aside, Newell's sharp mind and his ability to cut through the weeds meant what he had to say was always highly respected.

"The problem I have with this way of looking at things that way," said Newell, "is that people pat themselves on the back for superficialities. It's totally off-target. If there's a real problem and it needs to be solved to provide honest protection for people, then let's look at what needs to be done to solve the problem."

"Exactly," I said. "This is a federal government problem that exists because there's no communication between those responsible for America's strategic defense policy and those responsible for protecting America's population should anything unexpected happen. Rightly so, First Responders across the nation are the ones who will need to implement emergency response based on the direction coming from Washington. "So, the problem here is to get FEMA back on track."

Nods from others urged me to continue.

"It's not helpful to the Defense Department or State Department if FEMA is out practicing evacuations, signaling that it thinks we can protect our population and win a nuclear war. That sends a message that we might think of starting a war, absurd as that is. U.S. policy has always been that nuclear war is so unthinkable that we need the fear of Mutual Assured Destruction (MAD) to be credible enough so that no one would ever start such a war. You'd think these two federal bureaucracies could at least get their policies coordinated."

"So, let's see what's happened in the last two years," said Matthew, eager to bring this conversation back to our main focus of the newsletter.

"Is anything going on that might help get FEMA back on track?" Someone asked.

"I've got some of the notes here," Matthew said. "Why don't I just give you the highlights of what has been happening. Here's some of what people had to say: [3]

- A public meeting on the FEMA scheduled for Boulder, Colorado brought so many concerned citizens that it needed to be rescheduled. Even then, the rescheduled meeting in a local theater that seated 1,000 had a standing-room-only crowd. Lon E. Callen, Boulder's Director of Emergency Preparedness, had reported to his city manager in February, 1982, about the FEMA plan and the importance of telling the citizens about the disastrous effects of nuclear war and what First Responders were expected to do. The Boulder County Commissioners later turned down participation in the federal government's FEMA plan. "Inadequate protection," is why they said they rejected it. The *McNeill-Lehrer Report* covered the discussion quoting Boulder's Dr. Jack Geiger who said that the plans were dangerous for two reasons: 1) Soviet satellites would detect the population relocation sites and could attack them first to disrupt American homeland stability, and 2) the American public would be lulled into false sense of security thinking that the federal government really was protecting them.

- Selectmen from Gill, Massachusetts voted not to be a host community that would welcome the influx of citizens relocated from one of the larger cities. "I don't think the plan is anything we should be doing," one said. The group added that the FEMA plan is "one of the things that might trigger the Soviets into thinking we were preparing to attack and that they should also escalate by implementing their civil defense plans."

- Endicott City, Maryland, Civil Defense officials showed their community a film called "Protection is Possible." The film advised people to "dig a four foot L-shaped trench in your yard big enough to accommodate your family." The reaction wasn't what the sponsors had hoped. The audience broke into hoots of laughter.

- West Virginia Emergency Services Supervisor, Tom Carr, reacted to hosting everyone from Baltimore in a nuclear attack. "Consider the possibility of the local Kmart manager opening the door and finding 600 people waiting to come in and sleep on his floors and on his merchandise. In a lot of rural areas of West Virginia, which is where these people will be coming, there is essentially no sanitation."

"Talk about humor and tragedy as two sides of the same coin," interrupted Matthew. "All across the country one minor federal government agency, FEMA, has arrogantly issued directives to local government First Responders to move city populations to the countryside."

"It is hilarious," another agreed. Cartoons could be made of the overflow parking at Kmart, of the store manager trying to explain that his boss thinks he's running a private sector business and he can't let people camp inside or let them arbitrarily 'borrow' all the camping equipment. Think of the pictures of kids roasting marshmallows in Kmart's parking lot. So funny and the same time incredibly tragic."

Matthew continued:

"How do displaced people feed their families, get diapers for their babies or get medicines? Where do they make a bed that's protected from the weather and from those who might steal what little they have?"

I thought to myself that this might be a wake-up call for America's affluent who smugly believe that 'good fortune' is something to which they are entitled without ever thinking that people can be victims of other circumstances.

"And there's another thing," Matthew said. "How do people trying to earn a living running a business deal with the horrific disruption that displacing people causes? It's not just the Kmart Manager; it's everyone in our economy. Yes, we need to help out in a crisis, but we need government to think through what they demand before they destroy our entire economy."

Another thought crossed my mind. Of course, he assumes that the nuclear strategic explosion hasn't already destroyed the economy.

"I'm glad the West Virginia people brought this point to center stage," said Pam. "How can people in charge of something have such silo vision?"

"There are more examples from across the country," Matthew said. "Let me read some."

154

- Mayor Stephen R. Reed, Harrisburg, Pennsylvania, commented publicly in early 1982. "I would have very serious reservations about the federal government's ability to guarantee any rapid movement of large numbers of persons from population centers to distant 'receiving areas.'" Reed cited his experience with the Three Mile Island (TMI) nuclear reactor accident and cited the problems his First Responders would face. There'd be little advance warning, inadequate emergency personnel already deployed, parents seeking kids at school, invalids to take care of. He wrapped up his comments with a swipe at Washington stating that the federal government wants to cut dollars for mass transit and, at the same time they expect local government to oversee massive public evacuations.

- Marilyn Braun Greensboro-Guilford County Civil Defense Director, gave a speech in February, 1982, to a City Council in her jurisdiction. She announced her plan to remove all the fallout shelter signs. "They mislead public," she told local officials and FEMA. "My department has won awards for our emergency plans. We take our jobs very seriously and we work hard. But protecting the civilian population in a nuclear attack is very different. We have no protection today...for this threat. To ignore this threat, or to falsely misrepresent its consequences would be an intolerable deception on the people in Greensboro and Guilford Counties."

155

- In Shreveport, Louisiana, Caddo-Bossier Civil Defense Director C.L. Brewton told public the following in early summer, 1982: "The plan has problems, but it's better than nothing. The big question about FEMA's evacuation plan is 'what do we do afterwards'? If life did continue, it would not be life as we know it."

Newell stopped puffing his pipe and added a comment.

"THAT is the essential question, he said. We can all be pleased to hear the Civil Defense Director from Shreveport bring it up. He's a First Responder who clearly wants to believe that the people giving him orders are careful enough to give him accurate and helpful orders. He doesn't want to buy into the idea of challenging the chain of command. But he is very smart—smart enough to ask 'why didn't you tell us what to do once we have evacuated. Now what? Isn't that really what's important?"

Newell continued. "This is why the First Responders are so very very important. After the lofty scientists and diplomats and politicians have finished constructing the 'theory' of how we keep American freedom safe from Communism, we really do need the First Responders to do more than stand up and salute. We need them to speak up on whether the theory can be put into 'practice' and to dare to say 'it won't work'."

"Yes," I say. But what's really important here is that they are the only people who have a) the capability to say 'it won't work' because they are the people who run disaster preparedness programs, and b) they are the only people who will really say that 'it won't work' because they have no choice, they will be blamed if they keep silent and the crisis relocation plan doesn't safeguard the public. That's a powerful motivation and the only really credible one."

"I know it seems our list is endless," said Matthew. "But, there's more. You need to see what individuals all across America have done in a very short time."

- The City of San Francisco's response was to appropriate $30,000 to follow the Cambridge, Massachusetts lead in printing and distributing a booklet to all those on their tax roles indicating the kind of disaster that local folks would confront if there were a strategic nuclear weapon explosion and to inform them of the problems with FEMA's evacuation plan.

- In late 1982 voters in Cleveland approved an amendment to the Cleveland City Charter that would prohibit the city government from accepting or spending public funds for civil defense against nuclear war. Councilman Dale Miller stated: "It's not practical. It's a waste of public funds and therefore it should be prohibited."

- The Missoula, Montana, City Council passed a resolution in the fall of 1982 exhorting the Montana Congressional delegation to withhold federal funds for FEMA's CRP program, the acronym for "Crisis Relocation Plan for nuclear war.

- On May 30, 1982, *The New York Times* quoted James Moran, Vice-Mayor of Alexandria, Virginia. Moran declared it "asinine" and "right out of 'Alice in

Wonderland'" to evacuate Alexandria, Virginia to Webster Springs, West Virginia.

- In Minneapolis, Minnesota, a "civil defense drill" was held to test the viability of using the marked fallout shelters. They found that buildings were locked, safety guards were reluctant to allow people to enter buildings, and some of the identified fallout shelter locations were in fact buildings that had been demolished. In cases where entry was permitted to a labeled fallout shelter, frequently standards for holding a crowd of people were substandard. Consequently, Minneapolis officials in the Fall of 1982 asked the state Attorney General to remove all fallout shelter signs.

- In 1982 the U.S. Conference of Mayors asked that the organization's president establish a special task force to assess the validity of FEMA's current nuclear attack preparedness plan. Along with this request, they urged those spending money on this plan not spend more tax dollars until the said report was complete.

Randy Forsberg was also at Josie's party. She wasn't directly involved in the civil defense project because she was the originator of the "Call to Halt the Nuclear Arms Race"—the *Freeze* movement. But hearing about the U.S. Conference of Mayors action prompted her to note what was happening in a larger context.

"These last couple of years have prompted an incredible groundswell of concern about the new rhetoric favoring nuclear weapons arsenals. It's not only the Mayors concerned about public safety. It's the U.S. Conference of Catholic Bishops endorsing a freeze on the nuclear arms race. It's polls that indicate that now, in 1983, 72% of Americans support the *Freeze.* Then there's the amazing fact that the *Freeze* resolution passed the U.S. House of Representatives."

Randy Forsberg continued: "All these things happening concurrent to the outcries about FEMA certainly have contributed to a climate of support for saying to the government that while people want a strong strategic defense, they also want to be sure that no one is duping the public when it comes to protecting the homeland." [4]

Matthew resumed the litany of local reactions to FEMA's plan.

"Here's what happened in Maryland. I like the analogy between a dumb evacuation plan and a dumb water-sewer plan and how the latter would be dumped as bad—no super emotion about how one ought to do it even if it is bad."

- William H. Brill, County Council Member from Ann Arundel County, Maryland commented on the Councils rejection of the FEMA plan. "It isn't a heroic posture," he said. "If this is a dumb water or sewer plan, you would say it isn't the right thing to do. And we'd reject it. This is dumb. So let's take it off the books."

- Dr. Stuart H. Shapiro, Health Commissioner of City of Philadelphia, testified before the Philadelphia City Council in Spring, 1982. His concern is health, a bit different from those First Responders concerned about public safety and traffic. He said, "I came to state clearly and directly that there is no way, no plan, no gimmick, no illusion about protecting health during a nuclear war. It simply cannot be done."

- Charles Rule, Alexandria Virginia Fire Chief said in the *Washington Post*: "We're not equipped to handle mass evacuation. You can't get across the 14th Street Bridge at 5:00 PM, let alone in an emergency."

- Grand Forks North Dakota is home to 150 Intercontinental Ballistic Missiles (ICBMs.) It's a military town. On December 6, 1982, the Grand Forks City Council voted to direct the Mayor not to participate in the Civil Defense Crisis Relocation Plan (CRP) for nuclear war and to tell President Reagan and FEMA that they think our tax dollars allocated to CRP should be reallocated, either to be used for peaceful purposes or to be applied against the national debt.

I turn to my co-riders in the train car. "My apologies for how long this list is. Maybe the AMTRAK personnel will provide us with more food and drink while I go over a few more on this list—the few more that I can remember just now. Isn't it amazing how quickly First Responders across the entire U.S.A got the message about something as crazy as FEMA's plan? Local officials had no trouble sizing up the problem. They acted quickly to make clear that they wouldn't engage in something that was ludicrous and they objected to tax dollars being spent on it. Here's the last of this story. It will tell you how this all 'made change.' You do, I'm sure, agree with me that this is a vast collection of 'nickel and dime' efforts."

- Robert Fiedler, former Director of Civil Defense for Muscatine, Iowa, resigned his position and held a press conference on Pearl Harbor Day, December 7, 1982. He said to the *DesMoines Register*, "For the last four years I have been given information about how FEMA's CRP is going to work. The more information I got, the more I felt it wasn't going to work. I'm a Catholic and my bishops have said that nuclear war is immoral."

- In Spring, 1983, Fr. Michael McCarron, Pastor of The Church of Incarnation in Charlottesville, Virginia, refused to allow a FEMA official to inspect his church as a possible fallout shelter. He issued a statement. "Church buildings would be open to anyone in need in any emergency, but planning for this particular emergency allows people to think nuclear war is winnable." His Parish Council and the Bishop of the Richmond Roman Catholic Diocese supported him.

- Lake County, Florida, in 1983 moved ahead with their FEMA CRP plans, but with great reservations. Robert Lewis, Lake County Emergency Management Director said, "there'll be hell to pay if FEMA's tenuous assumptions aren't correct." He prefixed a disclaimer on his report to FEMA saying that local resources are insufficient to deal with the impact of such an evacuation.

161

Those interested in the Lake County site wondered how it could be designated as the evacuation location for 300,000 people from Orlando and from Tampa, when it is within 50 miles of the Crystal River Nuclear Power plant—a facility that might add to the problems because the radioactive materials within the nuclear power plant might well be released if a strategic weapon were detonated.

"That's enough for now," said Matthew.

Josie is overwhelmed with the short time it has taken to get the nation's First Responders to focus on a problem that needs fixing. "In less than two years, the problem with FEMA's Crisis Relocation Plan (CRP) spread through the offices of First Responders and local government officials in every state in the U.S.A.," she observed.

"Look what happened," said Newell. "The public's not so dumb. They care. The responses were swift, heart-felt and practical. People want to know that their government isn't playing with them when it comes to their safety."

"So this is progress," I say. "Those who need to know that there's a problem needing to be fixed now know. And, it's not really anything we did, they did it themselves. They knew when they heard the new FEMA policy that it was crazy. They just needed to know that they weren't the only ones who felt that way. But what's really important is to focus on how to correct the problem."

"Indeed," Newell said. "If people think no one hears them, that's when reasonable steps toward problem-solving break down. That's when no change is made."

Pam Kelly wandered over to our discussion to listen. "I'm interested in rural communities," she said. "So I just read a food and agriculture report. And I learned about something that you may be interested in. Iowa Congressman Tom Harkin really took on FEMA. Maybe some of those First Responders from Iowa reached him. But, then, he also follows the Arms Race issues and he is worried that the current administration rhetoric that seems to suggest nuclear arms race escalation could do harm to super-power stability."

"Tell us more about Harkin," someone says.

"Apparently, in 1983, FEMA presented a paper on "Food Vulnerability" to the Council on Food and Agriculture. Harkin attacked the FEMA report and is quoted in the December 6, 1983, *Washington Post* saying that "The misdirected perceptions of those involved in this briefing ought to shock us all. With information like this, it is no wonder that there are those in our government who believe that we can win a nuclear war." [5]

"Thanks, Pam," I comment. "You never know who picks up on an idea, who worries about a problem, or who wants to see it solved. Lots of 'nickel and dime' input from everyone who cares enough to take any initiative.

"There's something you may or may not know about." I added. "Beginning in 1982, FEMA started threatening communities who said they wouldn't take the CRP Planning money. Peter Koff, our lawyer, has been tracking this and the implications of it. *The New York Times,* June 6, 1982, reported on the City of New York rejecting the FEMA Crisis Relocation Plan for nuclear war 'protection'. The article mentioned that a spokesperson for FEMA threatened to terminate or withhold other emergency preparedness funding from communities that rejected CRP."

"Sounds to me," I continued, "like a typical reaction from an agency that might be threatened, or more likely, embarrassed. If you don't shut-up and take our money to do your evacuation plans in event of a nuclear disaster, we'll deprive you of the money we know you do want—the money for hurricanes and tornadoes and floods."

Newell jumped in. "Sometimes I think the 'Beltway' around Washington is a high wall preventing bureaucrats inside it from seeing the reality of what's happening across the nation that those in D.C. are there to govern. Can they really think that people across the country are dumb enough to tolerate that blackmail? Can they really think people aren't smart enough to know that FEMA got caught doing something stupid?" [6]

Matthew, who had taken over as editor of our newsletter after the first year, commented. "There's more. It's clear that FEMA is getting some grief for their plans. By May, 1983, FEMA's film and booklet, 'Protection in the Nuclear Age' had been withdrawn from public circulation. No comment about why. It's just gone!! And that's a very good thing."

"One more thing," Matthew said. "I was talking with Pete on the phone last week. You all know that Peter Dyke has now followed me as editor of our newsletter. We were delighted when he accepted our invitation to do so. It's been good to rotate the work because it's fairly time consuming and we're all volunteers; but it's also good to rotate location since this is a nationwide effort. Pete is a former CIA Senior Officer. He retired in 1975 to the New Mexico mountains after twenty-five years of postings in Europe, Southeast Asia and Washington, D.C..

"When we spoke," Matthew continued, "Pete was telling me how FEMA was trying one of the other classic game plans to recover from embarrassment. They were changing names and reorganizing offices. He told me how Congressman Boland from Massachusetts took FEMA to task at a Congressional hearing. It may have been the annual budget hearing."

Congressman Boland said, "name changes, aggregating program elements differently and slight changes in emphasis as not really substantive changes. I don't see where last year's plan has been substantively changed in civil defense."

Matthew then told us that Pete went on to say that, when New Mexico Governor Toney Anaya wrote President Reagan on December 20, 1983, to say that New Mexico would no longer participate in the Crisis Relocation Plan (CRP), it needed to be referred to as the Population Protection Plan (PPP.) Pete noted that the name-change-game had already reached the grass-roots.

"Pete wrote an article for our latest newsletter," added Matthew. "The new name for CRP is now Integrated Emergency Management System (IEMS.) Pete's article asks whether IEMS is intended as deception or whether it is the product of incompetence. Peter Dyke's answer is that it is both. The FEMA people remain too disconnected from any understanding of what nuclear weapons do to have any understanding that nuclear war is not just one notch up on the disaster scale from a flood or hurricane or tornado.

"But," Matthew continued. "The important thing to note here is that the message from the First Responders across the country is getting through to Members of Congress and to the FEMA executives that they need to change something. It's not acceptable to peddle this evacuation planning as protection for people in a nuclear attack. The families in America deserve better."

Through thousands of nickel and dime efforts, national change happened. It's not necessary to say who made the change or why. It's only necessary to know that people who refused to sit silent made a difference in ultimately ending the FEMA plan that dared to ask our First Responders to implement something that would never work and that the nuclear arms race saber-rattlers of the early 1980s eventually recognized the potential dangers of the plan's instability.

Josie Murray remembered one of the early quotes in our newsletter—from an Aaron Lansky in Amherst, Massachusetts. Lansky wrote: "The Holocaust was perpetrated by bureaucrats who forgot to ask why, who watched without comment. Having lost family and friends to one holocaust, I can not be content to sit by and watch a second holocaust. Are evacuation plans a placebo leading to a false sense of security the same way that evacuation plans and weapons stockpiles brought false security also to Germans on the eve of World War II?"

Pam Kelly said, "as a parent of young children, I'm certainly glad to find people who care about solving these problems that could be so detrimental to my two boys. So often I hear only from parents who see no relevance for their children in anything other than decisions about the latest toy in the store. They don't think beyond the school lunches and the after-school sports. How can smart parents be so short-sighted? At least some First Responders cared and dared to speak up—enough so that Washington couldn't ignore them and maybe our nation will uphold our trust and care about homeland safety."

Counterpoint Four

Humor, Networking and Self-Interest Can Make Change

Chug-a-chug-a-chug-a-chug-a-chug. Mile by mile our train is transporting us across the country. Certainly not as fast as it would have been by plane. Certainly not as easy, either. But we can walk around. And sometimes there's something to see out the window.

Richard, John, Paul, Ted and I are still talking in the Club Car. The bar is even closed now. It's late, but none of us can sleep.

Our conversation began when the trip started. The noisy group that left had been arguing about how things in America need to "change." They wanted a better job solving major international and national problems and complained that nothing got fixed fast enough. Their conversation reflected anger, frustration, and impatience. When they left, we five picked up where they left off, but in a more positive mode, moving from complaining about problems to solving them. The stories each tell about specific change-making. But more than that, they tell about the techniques that enabled success.

I had said that I'd spent several decades examining why, when, and how things change in public policy and that I thought it was deceptive to lead people to believe that change is a merely a soundbite command. You can't command change and expect instant results. It rarely works in any situation.

The five of us have very different views on how the world works, we agreed that we would discuss how, when if change works, with my providing my real-world examples for the others to critique.

I ask, "So what do you think about the story of the First Responders across the U.S.A. and changing FEMA's approach to safeguarding the public in event of a strategic nuclear weapons emergency?"

I'm eager to hear their views on this example of making change—the nickel and dime way–change first locally and then nationally.

Paul yawns. "I don't know why all those people bothered to try to change policy. I agree that the FEMA plan is pretty funny. Can't you just picture the little old lady digging a hole under her car? Or imagine being the manager of a big box store in no-where-ville and 600 people want to come into his store to sleep and eat and use the facilities—when he's not even open."

"But what difference does it make to change policy?" Paul continues. "Sure, it would be nice to know that we public are protected in the event of so unlikely an event. A nuclear disaster would really ruin my golf game on Saturday. And it might even screw-up my son's Little League game. But I don't know if that kind of accident will ever happen. I guess it's up to the government to keep us strong and safe."

"Paul, you tell us that you don't trust the government. You've been telling us all evening that government just wastes of your hard earned tax dollars. So do you trust them on the issue of homeland security now?" I ask.

Paul responds. "Well, the thing is that there's nobody else who can call the shots on national security. I just wish all those Washington agencies would speak with the same voice— especially when it comes to protecting me and my family. Like you said, it's a potential hazard for the very people we're trying to protect to have FEMA send us on a wild goose chase while the Defense Department strategic plan is all embroiled in nuclear arms negotiations with the Soviets and with spending money on our arsenal here in the U.S.A. I pay for them to get it together; I shouldn't have to blow the whistle and ask for a time-out so they can get it right."

"Who else, other than the American public, is going to provide the check and balance on getting it right?" Richard asks. Isn't that the difference between having a democracy and a dictator? Don't we do better when we keep seeking ways to improve what we do?"

John jumps in. "What right do people have to ask questions about national defense? This must be left to the people in charge. We elect them and then we've got to trust them. They have staff experts who have worked for years on these matters. That's how it goes; unless of course the winner comes from the political party that I don't like. Then, all I can do is complain and badger everyone I know to give the son-of-a-bitch a hard time so he can't accomplish anything and he's not reelected. We business leaders know how to get to someone who is screwing up. Those given a job like the one at FEMA will get it right. You've just got to trust us; we're your leaders."

"John," says Paul, "sometimes the people in charge do dumb things. Sometimes they try to bluff their way through and they are so protected that they really don't even know that the world knows they are screwing up. Hey, John, this isn't just about the FEMA guy in the story from the 1980s. Look at the terrible job that FEMA fellow made responding to Hurricane Katrina a few years ago. He didn't know he was screwing up; he was just riding in and out of New Orleans in a plane. Hell, the President couldn't even see what a mess it was. Remember the President congratulating him on TV, "You're doing a hell of a job, Brownie."

Paul continues, "Now, coming back to the story we just heard, what these guys do on their own watch is O.K. with me, but if they are spending my tax dollars to do it, or if they're doing things that might interfere with my kid's softball game, then I'm gonna tell them where to get off! Or, maybe I'll just bitch about it until Election Day so as not to interrupt my golf game. I guess if I don't know who to call or how to make change happen, I'll probably just join the crowd who is bitching. No choice—bitch or let it go."

"Besides, John," says Paul, "I don't like people who are smug and tell me that they know it all—just rubs me the wrong way."

"Actually I thought the story was pretty cool," said Ted. "Just think of the P.R. opportunities with all the humor and pictures of all of Philadelphia moving to West Virginia. Why you could have stories about local First Responders making sure that people with the wrong license plate didn't go on the wrong day. You could have tear-jerking stories about a family in the traffic line still trying to find their kid who left school but didn't get home yet. You could have hilarious pictures of some business security guard trying to keep the neighbors who don't have cars to evacuate out of the classy office building when the building has a fallout shelter sign. Great human interest. It's a cameraman's delight. Our audiences would increase. Our ad base would increase. Wow, what a moneymaker for my company. It would be better than the bucks I rake in at campaign time when each candidate is hitting the other over the head."

"Be serious, Ted," said Richard. "In a real emergency, your company would only lose—no electricity, staff scattered, property destroyed, no audience because people are too busy trying to survive. Think beyond the end of your nose. Think of media's self-interest long-run, not just short-run."

"Yeah, yeah, Richard," said Ted. "But putting my business first in-the-short-run is the way America has always kept rising to greatness. There's no time to think about the big picture, the long-run. My business I can count on; all this other stuff is beyond my control. I just have to deal with things as they come at me."

"Your media empire is more powerful than all those First Responders and the scientists and most of the people in the story," Richard says to Ted. "They made change, first one by one—nickel and dime change. Eventually what they cared about made so much sense to so many people that, thanks in part to their ability to ride the humor van to a spot in national headlines in every city and town, they changed national policy at FEMA. And all the media companies made money covering the stories; that's how the message spread to the point of changing national policy. So, how can you say that it's beyond your control to do anything about bigger problems?"

"What gets me," said Richard, is that all these First Responders sitting in their own offices, like all of us, are likely to wait a while before they speak up. They need to be cautious, as we all do. Nobody likes to blow the whistle because nobody likes the one who has blown it. These First Responders are just trying to do their jobs and protect the public. They fear being labeled as radical or not in the main stream. And that's what is likely to happen if they are the first to speak-up before anybody knows what they are talking about. To speak-up, you need cover. The public needs to already know the story and at least some segment of public needs to agree that the FEMA plan won't work."

"That's why is it that we just do what we did yesterday," Richard continues. "It cuts the frustration level to just keep on keeping on. Do your job. Don't ask questions. The problem is that we get to the point where we just 'believe' things without even thinking—just trust that FEMA and the feds will protect us. Is that laziness or fear? Is it ignorance? Have they all just been hypnotized?" Richard pondered. "I'm proud of those First Responders who stood tall and said the CRP plan wouldn't work. I think they stood up to make change because they knew they'd be blamed if they had to implement FEMA's plan. Plus, they got courage when they found out that their colleagues were also opposing the plan. Strength in numbers, you know."

"To make change meant that each of those individual people needed to take initiative, to have courage, to believe that speaking up was important to people's safety and also to their personal job success," Richard continued.

"Clearly the fact that the media had half the U.S. either laughing or crying helped," Ted added.

"What's important here is that self-interest always is a motive behind accomplishing change to fix errors and to achieve lofty ideals. However, self-interest alone would not have brought the change to the federal policy." I commented.

"We've become so specialized in the last few decades," I noted. "I think it makes it even harder for people to make change if they have to go outside 'their silo.' For example, here it was great because First Responders talked with First Responders and their bureaucratic counterparts in Washington. But it wouldn't have worked for the nuclear scientists to talk with the First Responders or vice versa; they speak different languages and have different experiences and do different jobs. The communication and cultural gap is too huge.

"I think that the fact that these recent decades of specialization and the new Internet communications have resulted in categorizing everyone into their own silo is and will continue to be a major deterrent to problem solving," I ponder.

"Are you game for another story?"

The Fourth Story—Coconut Road $10 Million Tainted Earmark

Local Elected Officials Give Tainted Money Back to Feds

CHANGE THROUGH LEGAL CHANNELS AND POLICY VOTES USING BUREAUCRACY, MEDIA & POLICY ENTREPRENEURS

"You know, those local government officials in Southwest Florida really did tell the 'Feds' to 'stuff it' when Washington tried to force them to take $10 Million for a project not in their Long Range Plan," said the radio host who was interviewing me for a mid-western radio call-in talk show.

"It's a remarkable story," I said. "Really it's two stories: change made locally demonstrating that local officials do have backbone–if they care to use it–and change made in the U.S. Congress because of national discontent with the practice of wasting tax dollars on 'earmarks'." [1]

The interviewer continued. "It seems to me that neither change could have happened without the individuals involved at both local and federal government levels, citizens taking the initiative to say that something was unacceptable, and they succeeded."

"You're right," I said. "It took three years, but we succeeded."

"What's the background? Tell me the whole story," the interviewer said.

"It'll take an hour to tell it," I said. "Your listeners will get bored."

"Not my listeners," she said. "They like political controversy, especially when the good guys and gals win."

"O.K.," I said. "Here goes. Basically it's the story of Alaska Congressman Don Young's arranging a $10 million boon for a Southwest Florida developer in exchange for $40,000 raised for him at a Florida fund raiser. It's the story of 'Coconut Road.' The Alaskan Congressman was, at the time, the powerful Chair of

176

the U.S. House of Representatives Transportation Committee. The 'Coconut Road' story is a sequel to Young's 'The Bridge to Nowhere' venture in Alaska."

A call-in listener interrupted: "A Congressman from Alaska getting a fundraiser in Florida? That doesn't make sense. Or is it about dollars and cents?"

"That's exactly the point," the interviewer responded, "and the proper cue to introduce my guest today. Carla Brooks Johnston, former Mayor of Sanibel, Florida, who, as Chair of the Lee County Florida Metropolitan Planning Organization, opened a Pandora's box of political chicanery that not only rocked Southwest Florida, but the United States Congress, the White House and the FBI. She says that one thing just led to another."

"You're pretty low-key about telling this story," the interviewer said. "You said not to call you Mayor or Chair, just to call you Carla."

"That's right," I said. "The importance of this story goes far beyond anything I did to trigger it. It's a template for how change can be made in political situations—and an indicator of all the moments where something could go wrong. We were more fortunate than an orchestra conductor might be; everyone did the right thing at the right time to get the right results, and we certainly had very little to do with orchestrating it. One doesn't orchestrate a group of elected officials. They are more independent than a herd of cats and fully aware of the consequences surrounding each step they may take."

"O.K., Carla," she said. "I want to tell our listeners the whole story of how change can be made in politics. I'm going to introduce the story by reading from the chronology of events that you gave me." [2]

"On August 24, 2005, as Mayor of Sanibel, Florida, and as one of the group of 15 local elected officials, who were members of the Metropolitan Planning Organization (MPO), the body charged with prioritizing and approving federal capital transportation expenditures in Southwest Florida's Lee County, I knew something was unusual when the MPO was informed that it was receiving a $10 million 'gift' for a Coconut Road Interchange, a project not on our list of priority roads. By 2007, the year the real Coconut Road story surfaced, I had become Chair of the MPO."

"This new provision was part of the 2005 Transportation Bill, known as SAFETEA-LU, which had been signed by President Bush. Consequently, the Florida Department of Transportation was directing the Lee MPO to amend its prioritized twenty-year *Long Range Transportation Plan* and its five year *Transportation Improvement Plan* to add the Coconut Road Interchange as a priority. Theoretically, all our funded projects must be justified in these voluminous documents based on traffic studies and growth areas."

The interviewer continued to read more of the report. "To the credit of the elected officials from Lee County and its municipalities, most members were asking questions. Some were angry at the mandatory addition of a Coconut Road Interchange saying that the mandate made our time and efforts in setting priorities a waste. Others thought that the Interchange project was unjustified, as shown by traffic counts and its proposed proximity to existing Interchanges. Some were concerned that such an Interchange would disrupt nearby suburban neighborhoods and would destroy abutting water conservation land. Others suggested that the Interchange was just a power grab by one segment of the business community at the expense of others in business and development because it was intended to increase the value of a particular abutting parcel, thereby making it easier for roof-tops to encroach into protected Everglades lands. Others worried that with dollars becoming increasingly scarce, the county's real priority projects would be delayed while the $100 million that it would cost to construct the complete Coconut Road Interchange siphoned off available funds from other projects. I was disturbed that we were unable to get a straight story of how we were allocated $10 million for a project that we didn't ask for and didn't want."

"That's a long explanation and the story has just begun," I interrupted. "Perhaps too much for your listeners?"

"Let's ask them," she said. Immediately the studio phones began to ring.

"I want to hear more," said a female voice. "Sounds like an approach we can use in our county."

"Keep going," said a male voice. "It's the beginning or a good political mystery story and I want to hear how it all comes out."

"O.K.," I said. "You do need the rest of the back-story because without understanding that you will never understand how it was possible to secure a majority vote of the entire Lee County MPO Board—the 10 elected city officials and 5 elected county commissioners—to ask the U.S. Congress to take the money back and give it to something people needed."

The interviewer continued quoting from my report.

"Based on the belief that we would lose this money—the $10 million we needed to allocate toward the widening of I-75—if we did not use it for the Coconut Road interchange project, we spent many MPO meetings discussing what possible alternatives there were. On September 23, 2005, we voted against putting Coconut Road into our *Long Range Transportation Plan*. Subsequently, the 2006 MPO Chair, John Albion, wrote U.S. Congressman Don Young, Chair of the House Committee on Transportation and copied our Congressman, Connie Mack, also a member of the House Committee on Transportation. He inquired about redirecting the funds to our priority projects. The two letters in response told Lee MPO Members they had no choice but to spend the dollars on Coconut. Johnston's report includes excerpts from these letters." [3]

The interviewer stopped. "How about you reading those letters, Mayor Johnston?"

"O.K." I read.

> "Projects for which funds are designated are available only for that project." (U.S. Cong. (R-AK) Don Young.) "….It does not appear the $10 Million for the Coconut Road interchange project can or will be re-programmed for other purposes, Second, if the MPO chooses not to utilize this $10 Million for this project, there is a reasonable chance that my colleagues in Congress will work to rescind the funds in light of the overall emphasis of reducing federal spending obligations. …..I am concerned that the MPO's vote will make it difficult for Southwest Florida to have future success in securing federal resources for other important projects." (U.S. Cong. (R-FL) Connie Mack)

"I find two things interesting," said the interviewer. "The language of the threat to withhold funds for other projects that is in the Mack letter is similar to the language issuing similar threats in the later Florida Department of Transportation letter in your report. Second, this Mack letter in your report is not signed, but simply has a printed "M" at the bottom. I believe that the original FDOT letter threatening to deny funds also was not signed. You later received a second letter after you requested from Washington that they clarify their threat and send a signed letter."

I complimented the interviewer. "It's nice to meet someone who does such thorough preparation for their show."

"I try to be very professional," she said.

The interviewer returned to my report.

"Concurrently, the then President of Florida Gulf Coast University, (FGCU), Dr. Bill Merwin, came to an MPO meeting to personally tell us that Coconut Road was important to the university, and later informed us that Congressman Young had personally told him that he supported this project."

"I have a copy of a letter sent by Mayor Johnston to President Merwin when he was soliciting support of local officials for Coconut Road," the interviewer said. "Here are some excerpts:"

"August 4, 2006

William C. Merwin, President, Florida Gulf Coast University

Dear President Merwin:

Thank you for your letter of May 17, 2006 concerning the Lee County Metropolitan Planning Organization (MPO) and the proposed FGCU Transportation Management Center.

Please know that I am heavily supportive of FGCU's Transportation Management   Center. As one who has spent a number of years engaged in University teaching as well as in public agency administration, (agencies focused on transportation planning), I imagine that such a center would be beneficial in many ways and that wide ranges of transportation interests would be able to finance its creation and able to help with its ongoing support. FGCU is unique in that its location is in the center of a rapidly growing metropolitan area. Surely this center will be critical to the research, development and application of a range of high tech transportation management techniques for all modes of transportation essential to the smooth movement of both people and goods. This of course, would include air, motor vehicle, bus, rail and water transport.

Given that multi-modal transportation is essential to the vitality of a prosperous metropolitan area,   I would be astonished to find you without funding for the proposed Transportation Management Center. It's in the interest of State, Federal and Private transportation to see it funded and certainly not to limit its usefulness to just one interchange.

Sincerely,

Carla Brooks Johnston, Mayor"

The interviewer continued with my report. "The letters from Congress stating that there is no alternative to spending the dollars on Coconut Road concerned me because it did not address our question of how we got the funds and how the funds could be reprogrammed to a priority need. I knew that other bills are corrected, so why couldn't this be corrected?"

Another listener phone call: "We can't get through the local bureaucracy to even get heard. How did you do it, Mayor Johnston?"

"That's a good question." I answered. "If you don't know who you want in which office, you can easily get a run-around from secretaries who may, in fact, not know enough about what happens up the ladder to know who to connect you to. You learn after a while to research who you want to contact before you call. And it never hurts to email specific questions so that you have specific written answers to your questions. It's best to start out assuming that those working in government might be normal people, like you, eager to do their job right. Not everyone in the bureaucracy is the enemy. Don't forget that when you asked me as Mayor how I got answers, I was at that time part of the bureaucracy. Although, over the years, I've seen how the public is handled from all sides."

"Just one other note on that topic," I said to the interviewer and the caller. "In this situation, the MPO—all elected policymakers with excellent access to staff members, who, in fact, worked for us—were taking a position quite unexpected for staff. Staff was not used for policy makers thinking independently. Staff held jobs requiring them to process certain documents and send the completed forms up the ladder to the comparable office in the state, which then sent their forms to the feds. There was no room in the staff work paradigm for variations on this procedure. Questions resulted in great nervousness on the part of staff. In our case, the MPO policymakers had made a decision we deemed correct from a policy view. Our staff looked at it totally differently. They worried that the state or someone up the ladder might cut off funds and they would be without a pay check."

"It's always about self-interest," I conclude. "You can never expect bureaucracy, or anyone else, to march lock-step."

The interviewer says, "Allow me to read some more of the report of the Coconut Road events." She continues.

"Although I, and most members of the MPO, believed that we needed to further explore alternatives in order to retain our priorities, our MPO staff and the Florida Department of Transportation staff believed that we had no choice but to include Coconut Road in the *Long Range Transportation Plan*. Several members of the MPO warned against turning our back on these funds. So we spent months trying to find ways to use this money consistent with our priorities, but not to fund an interchange study. At our April 21, 2006, meeting we voted to include in the study a model run on what would happen to traffic congestion if 8,000 housing units were built on the eastern side of I-75 as an expected result of a Coconut Road Interchange. Such work could quantify the negative impact on transportation flow, on water resources, and on smart growth attempts to balance development with encroachment into the Everglades. At MPO meetings in August, 2006, as well as April and May, 2007, the Metropolitan Planning Organization continued to discuss Coconut Road. Discussion of what to do with these dollars was taking too much time away from other agenda priorities. Most MPO members wished it would go away."

"How did you make it stay?" the interviewer asked me.

"It's not a question of making the dollars stay. It's a matter of law. The federal 2005 law appropriated $10 Million for a Coconut Road interchange. So the dollars are there. Either we start spending them for the legally mandated purpose or after several years the state might send the money back as unused or request the feds to reallocate the money in the next Transportation Bill, or we ask to use the dollars for something we needed and that the wording be corrected in the customary corrections bill that happens after most legislation is passed. The channels of operation that we call bureaucracy are both good and bad—depending on the circumstance."

The interviewer continued to read the report. "It became increasingly clear to me that 1) to spend these dollars on a Coconut Road Interchange would drain funds for priority projects elsewhere in the County, 2) to expand the study to serve those priorities was not really possible because of the wording of the federal law, and 3) to prolong this discussion was a waste of time because no one involved seemed able to answer the essential question of what legal options existed for us. I thought it critical that the funds go to our top priority— the widening of I-75. Southwest Florida is the fastest growing part of this state. Lee County has been increasing in population almost 5% per year during this decade. This part, as well as other parts of Florida, is a frequent target of hurricanes. Evacuating the population when hurricanes hit is a serious life or death matter. Our only Interstate I-75, with its four lane capacity, simply would not be able to handle such traffic. Even now, it's a parking lot in normal rush hours."

"By July, 2007, it also became clear to me that at our August meeting the MPO would likely vote on a finalized scope for the Coconut Road Interchange Justification Study and start to spend this $10 million earmark. We had been discussing with the Florida Department of Transportation (FDOT) what the scope of this study might be, with very little possibility of even tangential value to our real needs. As Chair of the MPO, I needed to protect our priorities. To prevent the Coconut Road project from becoming a fait accompli, I needed a substantive answer before our August meeting to the question of where the Coconut Road 'gift' originated and whether there was any way we could use the funds for something we really needed. I needed to find someone to research the matter, someone who knew their way around Congress and who was independent of the multiple currents within the MPO. I found that person in Darla Letourneau, a retired career federal employee who had worked both on Capitol Hill and in executive agencies as a liaison with Congress on budgeting issues. Her last position in Washington had been Deputy Assistant Secretary of Labor for Congressional and Intergovernmental Affairs."

Another listener phoned in: "It sounds like you didn't just keep tilting at windmills, didn't accept the letters from Congressman Young on face value, and didn't cave to the staff pressure to 'let it be.' In my view, it seems like the MPO and FDOT staff assume they are in charge and can wheel in the elected officials once a month to vote 'yea' or 'nay' on items as they wish. Is that right?"

"Yes," I said. "We hadn't followed the expected procedure. The local elected officials were taking the time to look at the facts and to vote in accord with what they thought was the self-interest of their cities and county. Here's more of what happened. I asked Darla to answer three questions: 1) Where did the money came from? 2) Is it possible to reallocate it to a needed project-widening I-75? 3) If it can be reallocated, how does one do that? She found what I wanted. We could get a technical correction. We could transfer the money to a priority project. It just would take a vote to do that from the entire U.S. Congress. We would not lose any of the funds until passage of the next Transportation Bill after 2009. A meticulous researcher, Darla Letourneau reviewed the FY2005 SAFETEA-LU Transportation Legislation and the over 6300 earmarks in that bill. She learned what no one yet knew nationally. Only ONE earmark, the one for the Coconut Road Interchange, had been added to the bill *after* Congress had approved the legislation and before the President signed it. This had been done by deleting the words that describe the purpose of the $10 million earmark from 'widening and improving I-75' and inserting the words 'Coconut Road Interchange.' Insofar as the U.S. Constitution and the House Rules state that Members must approve the content of a bill before it becomes law, this appeared to be a hi-jacking of the Constitution." [4]

A caller scoffed. "Hi-jacking the Constitution? C'mon. That's serious stuff."

"And it was taken seriously," I said. "On April 16, 2008, when this matter was finally resolved in the U.S. Senate, Senator Bill Nelson (D-FL) spoke on the Senate Floor about the needed technical correction for the Coconut Road project. Nelson said the following:" [5]

"A few years back, when we passed the Highway bill, they passed the version in the House, and we passed the version in the Senate, and they got merged so they were identical. The bill was getting ready then—the same bill that had passed both houses—to go to the President for signature. But a strange thing happened on the way to the White House because someone—identity yet unknown—went in and changed the language which was 'Widening and improvements for I-75 in Collier and Lee County'—a matter of $10 million in the highway bill—and changed that to be, instead, $10 million for a study for an interchange on Interstate 75 at Coconut Road...You simply cannot do that."

The interviewer added: "From the arrival of this 'gift' in Southwest Florida in 2005 to the ultimate correction of the problem in 2008, it required three years of hard work to actually make change—change only possible because hundreds of key elected officials, bureaucrats and media kept the matter focused and alive. From the Johnston report, here's what happened as this local story developed into a national story."

"Because Darla's discovery was a potential national bombshell, she double-checked the documents—all from original Congressional and Federal sources found on the web. She checked with D.C. congressional staffers, with *Transportation Weekly,* experts on transportation legislation, and with Taxpayers for Common Sense, public interest experts who comb through earmarks regularly. All were surprised at Darla's finding. None had caught the problem. All agreed that her research was correct. Her final report provided footnotes and attachments for every point."

An unexpected call to the studio came from a friend I knew in Florida. "I'm visiting my grandson up here," she said, "and

I just happened to tune in this program. I'd like to know how to return federal dollars that I think are a waste. But it sounds like even that's not easy to do. Can't someone just mail a check back?"

"Hi," I said. "What a nice surprise to hear from you. You're up in the mid-west where the show is originating, and I'm on my phone down here in Florida a few blocks from where you live and we're both on same radio show. With media connections I have a hard time figuring out when geography matters these days."

"Me too," said the caller.

"Let me comment on your good question—how can people send unwanted dollars back to Washington. The federal budget is huge and has many separate categories, each governed by laws and regulations. The laws and regulations have been put in place over the years because the public didn't want to just trust D.C. officials to do the right thing. So, that's good accountability. On the other hand, to return money has to follow the same funding categories and get the same approvals to remove funds from one place and put them into another place. More accountability, and with it more bureaucracy, more headaches, and delay. Bottom line, you can do what you speak of, but you need to follow a very clear roadmap. Let me tell you more of what happened in the Coconut Road story."

The interviewer summarized from my report:

"Several actions were important to getting the money channeled the right way after the local MPO voted to send it back. Johnston spoke about timing, distribution of the findings and getting bi-partisan support from Southwest

Florida's Congressional delegation without delay. She said that as soon as the Letourneau report was complete, she appended it to a press release given simultaneously to all SW Florida media for release a day before the MPO meeting to vote on whether or not to start spending the Coconut Road money. She said that great care was taken to deliver advance copies to the County Attorney, to each of the County and City Elected Officials who sat as the MPO, to MPO and FDOT staff, and to the offices of U.S. Congressman Connie Mack, and U.S. Senators Bill Nelson and Mel Martinez. She noted that to be successful in making change, it was essential to have no surprises for those whose support would be crucial. In addition, it was essential that there be full bi-partisan support for correcting the tainted earmark. The priority legal reason for eliminating the allocation for $10 million for Coconut Road interchange and allocating it to I-75 was based on the fact that the way it was inserted in the bill was illegal."

Before the interviewer could continue, another phone rang. "I'm a reporter," the caller said. "You know, we often don't think that strategically. We just spit out why someone is outraged rather than taking the next step of understanding what specifically, legally, and strategically is needed to change a policy and who is needed to get the majority support. It's a problem in our business when we're on deadline with a lot of stories to complete."

"That's true," I responded. "Let me cite some excerpts from the first releases on the tainted earmark written by the principal newspaper in Southwest Florida, *The News Press* reporter Ron Hiraki wrote the following article. [6]

"The $10 Million designated for the Coconut Road interchange study could be used to help widen Interstate 75 instead.

It's an option local officials will discuss August 17, now that a former federal official's report suggests that money might have violated the congressional process to create a highway bill.

The record appears to indicate that after all the votes from the House and the Senate were in, the change was made to the highway bill before it was given to the president, said Sanibel Councilwoman Carla Johnston, who requested the study...
Planning organization members continue to wrangle with the interchange, as they have for the past two years.

Opponents have argued special interests are driving the project, and that it would harm sensitive wetlands east of I-75 that are needed for drinking water, water cleansing, and wildlife habitat.

Supporters have countered the project would relieve traffic on congested Corkscrew and Bonita Beach Roads and that it has been discussed for 20 years.

The buzz has revolved around a Southwest Florida fundraiser that generated $40,000 for U.S. Rep. Don Young, (R-Alaska.) Young then set aside $10 Million for the project, which would boost the value of almost 4,000 acres east of I-75, land owned by developer Daniel Aranoff, who helped raise the money for Young...

'It wasn't until later that we learned it was specifically programmed for the Coconut interchange,' said Jeff Cohen, chief of staff for U.S. Rep. Connie Mack, Ft. Myers. 'It was money we did not seek nor did we know anything about.'

'It's just a political payoff to a campaign contributor,' Lee Commissioner Bob Janes said."

The interviewer then cites an article from another local paper. "Here are excerpts from Julio Ochoa's article in the *Naples Daily News*." [7]

"Report shows someone edited federal transportation bill. Young visited SW Florida in early 2005 to attend a town hall meeting. While in town, Daniel Aranoff, a wealthy part-time Naples resident who owns property east of Coconut Road and would benefit from the interchange, held a fundraiser for Young.

Many believe the fundraiser and Aranoff's financial influence were the reason Young alledgedly earmarked money for the interchange."

The interviewer continues. "It's often helpful to see what various papers say in reporting the same event. *The New York Times,* and *The Washington Post* also covered the local MPO story from August 17, 2007, as did other national press. Here's some excerpts from *The New York Times*" [8]

"'Congressman's $10 Million Gift for Road Is Rebuffed'

It is not often that a local government tries to turn down $10 million in federal construction money.....

The money for the interchange was the work of Representative Don Young, the Alaska Republican who was chairman of the transportation committee before the last election.

Officials of Lee County considered the project a low priority, environmental groups opposed it and the Republican congressman from the district never asked for it.

But the interchange, on Interstate 75 at a place called Coconut Road, would be a boon to Daniel J. Aronoff, a Michigan real estate developer with adjacent property who helped raise $40,000 in donations to Mr. Young at a fundraiser in the region shortly before Mr. Young inserted an earmark for the project in a transportation bill.....

On Friday, the members of the organization voted overwhelmingly to return the money in the hope that Congress would let them spend it elsewhere in the county.

Adding to the intrigue, a researcher commissioned by Ms. Johnston said Mr. Young had added the earmark for the interchange to a transportation bill after both chambers of Congress had approved it, at a time Congressional aides were cleaning up the bill for President Bush's signature.

'People were really highly outraged at the process,' Ms. Johnston said. 'It was a classic end run.....'

A spokeswoman for Mr. Aronoff, the developer and fundraiser, defended the project, saying a study had determined a need for the interchange in a building plan years ago, partly to help with hurricane evaluations....."

The interviewer added: "And here are some excerpts from *The Washington Post* Coverage on August 17, 2007. [9] Both national papers told the local story, but began to make the link to what would quickly eclipse the local story."

"'Fla. County Says 'No Thanks' to $10 million Earmark'

In a highly rare move, a local planning commission in Southwest Florida today overwhelmingly voted to reject a $10 million congressional earmark for a highway project, declaring that local officials never wanted the money in the first place...

As documented over the past few months by the *Naples Daily News,* Congressman Don Young (R-Alaska), who served as chairman of the House Transportation and Infrastructure Committee during the 2005 re-write of the national highway bill, took in $40,000 in campaign contributions at an event in February 2005 hosted by the developer. By the time the highway bill went to the White House in August 2005, a $10 million earmark had appeared for a new interchange off of I-75, known as the Coconut Road exchange. The developer owned property near the proposed interchange and would presumably build new homes on that land.

The county planning organization tried before to reject the money, citing other needs to expand different portions of the interstate to make hurricane evacuations easier. But the local officials were told the funds had to be spent on Coconut Road. "We were told we would jeopardize our future funding. ... Along came this gift of $10 million for Coconut Road, and it wasn't anywhere in our needs," **Carla** Johnston, a member of the county's MPO, told Capitol Briefing in a phone interview...

Former U.S. Labor Department congressional liaison, Darla **Letourneau,** ... investigated the Coconut Road earmark. Letourneau reported last week that the earmark, as passed in the final version of the highway bill by the House and Senate in late July 2005 included broadly worded language allowing for the $10 million to be spent on "widening and improvements in I-75." But during what Congress calls the "enrollment process"–a time for cleaning up any basic mistakes in the bill before sending it to the White House–the earmark was changed to designate the funds for "Coconut Road interchange/I-75..."

Rep. Connie Mack, (R-FL), who represents the county, has pledged to work with to make the changes.....

Keith Ashdown, an earmark specialist at Taxpayers for Common Sense, said he could not recall any similar situation in which towns or counties rejected such a big earmark.

Young has not commented on the Coconut Road earmark. When a *New York Times* reporter sought to ask him questions in June, Young made an obscene gesture at the reporter.

Young is under investigation by the Justice Department for his ties to an Alaskan energy services corporation, whose former CEO pleaded guilty in May to bribing five state legislators and other unnamed public officials. Separately, a former top aide to Young on the Transportation Committee pleaded guilty to accepting illegal gifts from now imprisoned lobbyist Jack Abramoff.

Johnston declined to address the issue of what the county organization will do if it cannot get the law changed. 'I am highly optimistic,' she said."

The interviewer adds, "I have one more press clip from August 2007. *McClatchy Newspapers* [10] posted an article from their perspective of following the national story more than the local one.

"'Federal investigation targets Alaska's congressman'

WASHINGTON — A Justice Department corruption task force is investigating whether Alaska Congressman Don Young took campaign cash in return for securing $10 million for construction of a proposed Florida highway ramp that would give a windfall to a local real estate developer, a source familiar with the inquiry said Friday....

It is among a number of congressional ``earmarks" for specific pet projects drawing scrutiny from the Justice Department and an FBI team investigating alleged influence peddling on Capitol Hill, said the source, who insisted upon anonymity because of the sensitivity of the matter. As the powerful chairman of the House Transportation and Infrastructure Committee from 2000 to 2006, Young added earmarks worth tens of millions of dollars to transportation spending bills.

Investigators' interest in the Florida earmark stems in part from its timing. In the two weeks before and after the earmark was inserted in the spending bill, Young's campaign and political action committee collected contributions from the Florida developer, Daniel Aronoff, and Aronoff's lobbyist as well as a number of other Florida business executives. The Florida donations, mainly from real estate interests, totaled more than $40,000.

Meantime, transportation planners in Lee County, the Gulf Coast community where the interchange would be located, voted Friday to ask Congress to let them use the money instead to widen Interstate Highway 75. They said they had never asked for the interchange money....

A former aide to Young on the transportation committee, Mark Zachares, pleaded guilty last spring to conspiring with disgraced lobbyist Jack Abramoff to buy influence in Washington.

As part of his plea agreement, Zachares admitted helping Abramoff in 2004 to win support for a separate highway project to benefit an unidentified businessman. He now is cooperating with investigators.....

Young was approached by leaders at Florida Gulf Coast University, which wanted the interchange for better access, said Young's chief of staff, Mike Anderson. School officials also wanted it to serve as a demonstration project for a sophisticated transportation hub that could be monitored with cameras during hurricane evacuations.....

Local transportation planners voted Friday to do just that. They want the money to go toward the overall widening of Interstate 75, not for the specific interchange, said Carla Brooks Johnston, who leads Lee County's Metropolitan Planning Organization....

Many in the community felt it would open up for development environmentally sensitive land owned by Aronoff, a longtime family friend of Young's who organized a March 2005 fundraiser in Bonita Springs, Fla., for the congressman.

The university's Washington lobbyist is listed as Rick Alcalde, a Young campaign donor and the same lobbyist who worked in Washington on behalf of Aronoff's firm, the Landon Companies.....

The $286.4 billion transportation bill included $24.2 billion for 6,371 special earmarks, said Keith Ashdown of the nonpartisan government watchdog group Taxpayers for Common Sense. It was "one of the most earmarked bills I've ever seen," Ashdown said. At least $2.5 billion of that money went toward projects in the districts of four top GOP lawmakers at the time, including Young."

I interrupted the interviewer. "Let me tell you a bit more about what happened at the local level in August, 2007. It may be useful to people from other places wondering what it takes to make change. By the time of the August 17, 2007, MPO meeting, the media had widely publicized what had happened. Over a hundred citizens came to the meeting. Each member of the MPO had received over 250 e-mails on the topic. Most of the elected officials were furious. The MPO voted 10-3 to send the $10 million back to Congress in order to clarify which project was, in fact, authorized. One of the elected officials on the MPO said the following to me. "It's nice, for a change, to see policy makers able to make policy. We never get to do that. Florida Sunshine Laws prohibit elected officials from talking to each other about topics on the policy table."

"I'll read some more of your report," said the interviewer.

"Our Congressional delegation, Congressman Connie Mack IV (R-FL 14), Senator Mel Martinez (R-FL) and Senator Bill Nelson (D-FL) had been informed of the tampering and they'd been given the Letourneau Report prior to the MPO meeting. The afternoon after the meeting, each was sent my formal letter on behalf of the MPO requesting that they find a way to return the $10 million to what they all had voted for—I-75 improvements. They would have it knowing the exact MPO request, and they would have material needed to make an intelligent comment when the press called them. All three officials replied in writing that they were committed to correcting the error."

The interviewer interjected, "here are excerpts from Congressman Connie Mack's August 21, 2007, response to MPO Chair Johnston's August 20, 2007, letter. Note that he responded within twenty-four hours. Time was not to be wasted in correcting this problem." [11]

"Pursuant to the Lee County Metropolitan Planning Organization's request, I have contacted House Transportation and Infrastructure Committee Chairman James Oberstar and Ranking Member John Mica seeking their support and assistance in restoring the House and Senate passed language to 'widening and improvements for I-75 in Collier and Lee County.'

As my staff has previously discussed with you, we will work hand-in-hand with the MPO as we attempt to restore this language. I am also aware of Senator Bill Nelson's interest in this matter and have directed my staff to coordinate this effort with his office as well."

The interviewer continued from my article the chronology of the process to make the change required to correct this tampered earmark.

"October 1, 2007, Congressman John Mica (R-FL), the Ranking Member of the Transportation and Infrastructure Committee wrote to our Congressman, Connie Mack (R-FL). He said 'I support your request and pledge to work alongside Chairman Jim Oberstar (D-MN) to ensure these funds are denoted for 'widening and improvements for I-75 in Lee and Collier County, Florida as it was originally intended when

Congress passed the 2005 SAFETY-LU Legislation on July 29, 2005.' Johnston described the incremental involvement of other key Congressional leaders—the Republicans to support Congressman Mack who many felt, as a new Congressman, had been used by Alaska's Congressman Young, the Democrats to champion the growing momentum in opposition to earmarks. Bi-partisan leadership in the Florida delegation was on-board! That was crucial in this game of hardball. It's the U.S. Congress alone that can fix the earmark problem. Nothing will be accomplished there if the item is buried in partisan wrangling."

The interviewer continues Johnston'sreport then tells more of the back-story of those who didn't want the earmark 'gift' derailed.

"Advocates for the Coconut Road Interchange were not happy. They included those who might benefit from the development of the 4,000 acres of water conservation land owned by developer David Aronoff directly to the east of the proposed Coconut Road Interchange. Others opposed the MPO action on the grounds that it was foolish to send needed money back to Washington even if the money was tainted. Some others were concerned that the rejection of the Coconut Road money might cost them their current or anticipated jobs. Some local bureaucrats opposed the MPO decision on the grounds that 'business is always done this way.' Apparently they had staked their careers on going along to get along regardless of logic or data or ethics."

Her report continued, "In the following months, efforts were made to reverse the MPO vote. Some of those efforts appeared to be attempts to intimidate local officials, including MPO members. One objection made was that the motion I had offered on August 17th, 2007 had not followed the customary protocol of prior review by MPO advisory committees—particularly the 21-member Citizen Advisory Committee. Several hundred citizens were ultimately involved in the deliberations and the media had covered the issue widely. In addition, for almost two years, the advisory committees had been part of this ongoing debate. It was critical for the MPO to act in August. Had we waited a month to convene advisory committees, the Coconut study would have been approved and by expending funds from this earmark, it would no longer be possible for Congress to correct the bill enrollment error as the MPO requested of our congressional delegation. Several factors were involved in the pre-emptive August action: 1) DOT guidelines stipulate a 'continuous, comprehensive process,' and that had been happening and would continue to happen. 2) Precedents existed where decisions were made with ongoing subsequent debate occurring within advisory committees and document changes made 'after the fact.' 3) Hundreds of citizens already had been clearly involved."

A call-in came from someone who said they were traveling out west when this story broke. "Didn't I see something in *TPMMuckraker.com* about the wife of a local developer who helped plan the fundraiser for Young being on your 'citizen' committee? I remembered it because we have a problem where I live of special interests who favor certain developments trying to get appointed to citizen committees and thereby stacking the citizen committees and not letting us really hear from Joe and Mary Citizen about their neighborhood."

"Yes, you have a good memory," I say to the caller. "*TPM Muckraker.com* did reveal what some might consider a conflict of interest for a Citizen Advisory Committee. [12] Here's what they wrote:

"To be fair in our coverage of Rep. Don Young's (R-AK) controversial $10 million

Coconut Road interchange earmark, we should point out that there are locals who want to keep the extra-Constitutional language change. One of the more vocal advocates also appears to have a financial stake in the decision.

Last week when county authorities voted to ask Congress to use the money to widen Interstate 75, rather than for the pet project, there was some opposition. Heather Mazurkiewicz, who belongs to the citizens advisory board, which advises the Metropolitan Planning Organization, supported keeping the changed wording. According to *The News Press* she was appalled that the county ignored her advice:

'I should be able to discuss the merits of this without a bias from you,' she said. 'We make recommendations to you. You don't make them to us.'

As it turns out, Mazurkiewicz is married to a consultant who pushed for the project and attended the fundraiser that netted Young $40,000 right before the earmark appeared. Joe Mazurkiewicz spoke with the *New York Times* and CNN about the fundraiser and the funding. In his initial interview with the *Times*, Mazurkiewicz was a bit more candid about the fundraiser, saying he and other developers were looking for 'a lot of money' and Young delivered. According to Young's contribution records, the Mazurkiewiczs gave Young's campaign $1,000 a few weeks after the February 2005 fundraiser."

The interviewer cited another attempt to make local officials back down from Johnston's report.

"On September 5, 2007, I received on behalf of the MPO an unsigned letter from the Federal Highway Administration (FHWA)'s Florida Division. The letter advised us that all federal highway, transit, and emergency relief, including hurricane recovery money, funds for the entire state were in jeopardy because the citizen advisory committee did not meet before we voted to block spending for Coconut Road. It was still hurricane season. In Florida one doesn't play games with hurricane recovery. Darla and I gave the letter to transportation officials in Washington who were outraged by this state FHWA letter and brought the matter of the unsigned letter to the attention of U.S. Department of Transportation officials in Washington. A subsequent *signed* letter dated September 9, 2007, came to me from FHWA making it very clear that since the MPO committees were meeting in September, our decision about Coconut Road was our business, and hurricane funds were never a matter for threats."

"The MPO subsequently received a letter from a Patrick Reilly, a Washington attorney. It had been sent to Florida Gulf Coast University for delivery to the MPO. It stated that we needed to carry forward with Coconut Road and not hope for a technical correction. An article about this attorney's letter appeared in the September 22, 2007, Ft. Myers, *The News-Press.* That article identified Reilly as a registered lobbyist and attorney representing Potomac partners, the D.C. firm working for both FGCU and for Aronoff's firm, Agripartners. Reilly's assumption must have been that local officials in Southwest Florida were not very bright. His letter appeared to be a tutorial on the three branches of government. It did not appear to stem from any extensive expertise in Congressional processes. It did not address the relevant points about the issue of making substantive language changes in legislation after Congress had voted."

The interviewer then commented on my report.

"It's amusing because those who want to spend the $10 million earmark for a Coconut Road interchange kept sending emissaries whose prestigious titles are supposed to cause local officials to bow in submission. After all, locals are at the bottom of the pecking order. The irony is that they have all this power that they abdicate to staff or to those 'wise' experts from Washington. As Johnston points out, locals have long been considered irrelevant except to the few who understand that they are the heartbeat of democratic policy making. Locals always cave, don't they? Not the majority of the 15 officials on the Lee MPO. And while Johnston's leadership and strategic sensibilities as Chair were critical to the success of this local rejection, Johnston could never have succeeded in stopping the spending of the tainted earmark without the majority vote backing of her local colleagues, and the widespread local and national media coverage that stiffened the backbone of those who needed to vote at the MPO early on."

The interviewer then turned to the next item in my report, comments on the next person sent to sway we misguided local officials. [13]

"Jack Schenendorf, an attorney at Covington and Burling, a leading Washington law firm hired by Agripartners, was flown in from Washington to attend the September 28, 2007, MPO meeting. To establish credentials at the beginning of his testimony, I asked Schenendorf to answer on the record whether or not he made campaign contributions to Congressman Young. We already had proof that he had contributed to Young, but it was important to hear him say it himself. He acknowledged that he did support Young's campaigns. One of the MPO members supportive of using funds for Coconut Road questioned the relevance of my seeking this information, but the point that Mr. Schenendorf was not independent has been made. No need for further discussion. Schenendorf's memo and presentation defended the earmark change taking money from I-75 and reallocating it to Coconut Road. He did not speak to the violation of House Rules. House Rules state on page 302, section 576 that 'Enrolling clerk shall make no change, however unimportant, in the text of a bill to which the House has agreed.' He made other questionable comments, including an assertion that the funds could not be reprogrammed, reallocated or transferred—a statement that would have been correct had he included the phrase 'without a statutory change.' It should be noted that all the members of our Florida congressional delegation had, before the Schenendorf statement, indicated in writing that they were working on a statutory change. The credibility of the Letourneau Report remained intact.

And, equally important, the bipartisan commitment of our Congressional Delegation to solve the problem of this tampered earmark was solid."

A call-in came from a man who said, "It's amazing and amusing to note the unimaginative techniques used by major powers to convince those with less power that they should line up and behave. Bring in a prominent lawyer with good titles and put him in a perfectly groomed pin-striped suit. Have him spout all sorts of legal language that is intended to impress the locals that they can't match this 'wisdom.' Be careful not to address the specific charges brought by the locals who don't want to rubber-stamp policy. What's amusing about this is that the high powered professionals have no idea how transparent this technique is. Why weren't they more imaginative?"

"That's a good observation," I say. "One problem we have when working to fix the broken parts of government is the disconnect between Washington and the local communities across the nation. Those who spend all their time in Washington seem to believe the arrogance that frequently accompanies the lofty titles and weighty jobs. They forget that we have a pretty well educated population. We don't always get that population to pay attention to key civil society issues, but when we do, don't underestimate them!"

"Let's finish the   chronology of this story," said the interviewer. She read from my report.

"At the September 28, 2007, MPO meeting I worried that some MPO members may have felt pressure to change their votes and might reverse our previous decision. In addition, I knew that the City of Ft. Myers delegation, three of our fifteen members, and three who had voted to send the $10 Million back, would be absent. The Red Sox spring training headquarters is in Ft. Myers and the entire Ft. Myers MPO delegation had been scheduled for a year to be in Boston this particular week to celebrate the team's winning the American League Pennant. In spite of their absence, the earlier MPO decision not to go forward with the Coconut Road Interchange study was upheld. That was a victory, a second vote confirming our message to send the money back."

The interviewer then noted that those seeking to derail our efforts to return this earmark then decided to try to discredit the key leaders and read from my report.

"I, personally, became a target for those opposed to the MPO action. First, there were two Freedom of Information requests from Heather Mazerkowitz for all my e-mail and phone records for the relevant time block. Nothing was found to be inappropriate. Then it was found that a house I owned in Cambridge, Massachusetts, was taxed at a resident rate instead of a non-resident rate. I learned about this in a front page headline in the *News-Press*. A 'gottcha' type article attempted to turn this into a scandal and referenced a letter allegedly sent to me by the Lee County Tax Assessor's Office threatening rescission of my Florida homestead exemption. The letter turned out not to have been sent—until later, after I challenged the Assessor's Office about the games happening with the newspaper. When the letter did come, it came from the Public Relations department, not from the department in charge of homestead tax status. Unsigned letters and letters sent from the wrong office appear to be one way to send threats, but not be caught doing anything inappropriate. Because I had not sold my home in Massachusetts when I moved to Florida, I did owe the city money. It was total oversight. I had changed addresses on tax returns, voting records, and my driver's license. But, I never called the Cambridge Tax Assessor's Office. It never occurred to me. I paid Cambridge the $9,000 balance due on that property tax bill. But the message implicit in how the supporters of Coconut Road launched this 'attack' was to create a scandal, to attempt to destroy reputations, and to make it known that officials who don't play as expected will be hounded and punished. I sent an article to *The News Press* thanking them for finding my error, noting that I paid the dollars due to the City of Cambridge, and commenting on the interesting coincidence of timing and PR 'hype' with attempts to intimidate opponents to Coconut Road."

"Johnston's report then noted an interesting change," said the interviewer. "After that MPO's second vote, Coconut Road, like a butterfly, began a metamorphosis whereby the caterpillar of multi-legged local political problems and the totally different national problem of Congressional Earmark politics turned one story into two stories."

A caller jumped in. "You know, I'd bet that the media would be much more interested in Congressman Young and the tampered earmark. Earmarks are getting to be a matter of controversy in Washington, the way to dish out the pork, you know. And anything controversial is magnified a thousand-fold come election season. Did that happen here?"

"You bet," I said. The national media loved the story. The juxtaposition of Alaska's snow fields and icebergs with Florida's beaches and coconuts were an opportunity for the media not to be missed. In January, 2008, *The New York Times* used the title 'Congressional Mystery: Quid Pro Coconut' for one article. [14] Here are some excerpts:

"Congressional Mystery: Quid Pro Coconut

One of the big themes in this year's presidential election, in both parties, is that things need to change in Washington. Exhibit A for that could be the the Coconut Road project in Florida...

It came about because Representative Young — Congress's pork-meister extraordinaire — passed through town on a fund raising mission and, after netting $40,000 from local developers, customized a budget bill earmark for them: $10 million to build a new interchange they wanted at Coconut Road. The route would boost developers' property values and, local officials warned, greatly harm the environment. It had echoes of Mr. Young's own home state "Bridge to Nowhere."

So far only Senator Tom Coburn, Republican of Oklahoma, seems to care. He is demanding to know who ordered the lawmaking process gamed after the decisive vote, rightly warning colleagues that this sort of trickery could happen again to even more important legislation that Congress thinks it has locked into law.

There's one other mystery concerning the Coconut Road project: why no one except Senator Coburn is outraged enough to demand that Congress investigate how its pocket was picked from within."

I noted that Senator Tom Coburn (R-OK) made national headlines in late December when he announced that he was holding up consideration of the Technical Corrections bill until the bill was amended to require a full and open investigation into the Coconut Road earmark scandal. The Lee County MPO's job was mostly irrelevant at this point, except that we needed to make sure that our actual technical correction for use of the $10 Million to Coconut Road wasn't forgotten. If a correction were not included in a Technical Corrections Bill, the Coconut Road Interchange could actually move ahead toward construction, despite the fact that the nation—its political leaders and its media–decried that possibility. To that end Darla's familiarity with Congressional staffers became enormously valuable. She filled two roles suited to her, the constant networking with those staffers in key leadership offices and providing regular updates to key media nationally. My role, as a local elected official, shifted to one of strategy discussions with Darla and keeping the MPO in the loop.

The interviewer broke in.

"In late September 2007, Taxpayers for Common Sense, a Washington watchdog group, sent a formal request to the House Ethics Committee calling on them to investigate the Coconut Road earmark.   Keith Ashdown, a researcher for Taxpayers of Common Sense, a Washington, D.C. watchdog group, stated the following:"

"This goes beyond the intent of the technical corrections process. It's supposed to be about getting your punctuation right, not about making sure that your major benefactor is getting their pork. The correction process can often be rushed, between the bill's passage and its signing. The change was made on page 367 of the 800-page bill. This is not how the process is supposed to work. I've seen little gimmicks and little tricks used to make sure somebody's friend or contributor is taken care of but this is by far one of the more underhanded, surreptitious examples I've seen — ever."

I added that this action raised the profile of the issue in Congress. *Transportation Weekly*, a highly regarded national newsletter for transportation experts in Washington and across the country, covered the story and dug deeper into its background from September, 2007 on. *Transportation Weekly's* April 23, 2008 editorial explained why the publication had covered it so extensively:

"The purpose we tried to serve by giving the project so much ink was twofold: to draw as much negative attention to the enrollment aspect as possible, so as to make it politically radioactive for any legislator or staffer to attempt such an enrollment change in the future, and to get Congress to put new procedures in place for the decidedly non-transparent bill enrollment process so that problems like Coconut Road...don't happen in the future."

I explained that media coverage kept fueling the earmark fire with Coconut Road being the poster child for what Congress does wrong. One more example is the following excerpt from syndicated columnist George Will's article published across the nation in February, 2008. [15]

"Coconut Road leads to waste, corruption"

There are two mysteries: Who surreptitiously perverted the will of Congress? And why is Congress not angry and eager to identify the culprit? It seems reasonable to suspect that the answer to the first question is: Young or an agent of his. The answer, or answers, to the second question probably is, or are: Because Young is powerful–and perhaps also because such violations of legislative due process have been committed on behalf of other members...

Fortunately, Senate rules enable an obdurate individual to force the institution to sit up and take notice. One such mechanism is a "hold," by which a senator can halt a bill. Freshman Sen. Tom Coburn is an Oklahoma Republican who happily has not learned the Senate ethic of playing nicely with others. He has put a hold on the bill that corrects technical problems in the 2005 highway bill..."

The interviewer then read the part of my report that chronicled the last stages of national involvement in Coconut Road.

"In early April, 2008 Senator Barbara Boxer (D-CA), Chair, and Senator James Inofe (R-OK), Ranking Member, of the Senate Environment and Public Works Committee had reached committee agreement to send the Technical Corrections Bill, HR 1197, to the floor for a vote. It now included the corrected language for Coconut Road, as formally requested by Senator Nelson and Senator Martinez."

"Ordinarily, that might be the end of the matter. But it was really only the beginning. In April, 2008, consistent with his December, 2007, statements, senator Coburn announced that he would offer a floor amendment to the bill (H.R. 1197), which called for the creation of a bicameral, bipartisan special committee to investigate when, how, why, and by whom improper revisions were made to the Coconut Road earmark. Senators Nelson (D) and Martinez (R) signed on to Oklahoma Senator Coburn's (R) amendment. All three Senators who were candidates for President—McCain (R-AZ). Obama (D-IL) and Clinton (D-NY)—also indicated support for investigation into the Coconut Road earmark. On April 15, 2008, Senate Majority Leader Harry Reid (D-NV) called for a Department of Justice investigation into the changing of the 2005 Transportation Bill after Congress had voted." [16]

"On April 16, 2008, the Technical Corrections Bill for the 2005 Transportation Act came before the Senate including the words needed to remove the $10 Million for Coconut Road and reallocate the $10 Million to widening I-75 tucked into a specific sentence within the lengthy bill text. On April 18, 2008, C-SPAN covered the discussion on the floor of the U.S. Senate, all focused on the discussion of Coconut Road and the tampered earmark.

As I watched it, I felt as if I were in a Rod Serling "Twilight Zone" episode, reviewing my own role and experiences in lighting the match that led to this moment in Congress. Senator Coburn offered his amendment requiring a congressional investigation. Senator Barbara Boxer (D-CA) offered an alternative amendment that required the Department of Justice to investigate Coconut Road. *The New York Times* reported on

April 18, 2008, that Boxer stated "I think it very possible people ought to go to jail here….a Senate and House committee can't send anybody to jail." To bring the debate to a conclusion, Senate Majority Leader Harry Reid (D-NV) and Senate Minority Leader Mitch McConnell (R-KY) agreed to set a 60 vote threshold to sort out which amendment would prevail. The Senate voted 64-28 in favor of the Boxer amendment—a strong bipartisan statement. This action appears to set a precedent, in that one branch of government (Legislative) has asked another branch (Executive) to investigate it, and in this instance the Senate is asking for an investigation of the House. After approving the Boxer amendment, the Senate voted 88-2 to pass HR1197 and restore the $10M to I-75." (Those interested can read the full *New York Times* [17] and *The Washington Post* [18] coverage from April 16-18, 2008 as well as the articles in *The Hill* [19], *Congressional Quarterly* [20] and *McClatchy Newspapers* [21] and the transcription of the proceedings of the U.S. Senate debate in the *Congressional Record* [22].)

I then described the end of the Washington story.

"Shortly after Senate passage of the bill, House Speaker Nancy Pelosi (D-CA) announced that the House that she supported the Department of Justice probe, and suggested to reporters on April 17th, 2008, that the House Ethics Committee should also look into this matter. House Minority Whip Roy Blunt (R-MO) also supported the Senate-passed bill and said in response to a reporters question that he 'always said there should be an investigation and that is still the case.' On April 30, 2008, the Senate-passed bill, H.R. 1195, was adopted by the House under its Suspension Calendar, which means that no amendments are in order. The bill went to the White

House where the President signed it into law. The circle was now complete: the $10 million was now designated for I-75 widening and improvements, as in the original Congressional vote."

The interviewer asked if I had any final comment.

I replied, "Nelson Polsby, author of *Policy Innovation in America,* pointed out that innovation never happens without the interplay of four things: an incubation period, a crisis, good timing, and policy entrepreneurs. The Coconut Road caper certainly has all of these ingredients at both local and federal levels. Timing, it must be noted, could not have been better. The developing of solutions to the Coconut Road earmark are coincidental with a presidential election, a time when neither Republicans nor Democrats can tolerate corruption, or at least, the appearance of corruption."

She gave the final word.

"I believe in this time-consuming process of working with the laws and official records. We are not a country of people's opinions. We are a country of laws because that is the most fair way to make our decisions."

Counterpoint Five and Conclusion

The System Can Work If the Public Can Figure Out What's Possible

"Wow," says Ted. "That Coconut Road Earmark story is a movie! It's a great mystery, adventure, conspiracy, political maneuvering. All you need is for Hollywood to spice it up a little, a few less procedural maneuvers and a bit more sex and violence and you've got a good show."

"But" I say, "what happens to the 'real world' when people shift the story into the 'entertainment world' fantasy? There's got to be a way to tell a story that keeps people's interest in wanting to improve their own condition—such as not to be over-taxed and under-served."

I continue. "People yell, scream, march, sign petitions, send text messages because they are outraged when government does something wrong or when they just get fed-up. Are you telling me that when it comes to fixing what's wrong, people can only be interested if it's fantasy and not the real world?"

Ted replies. "It's not my job to think about that. It's my job to use all these neat technologies to keep people wanting to pay my company. To do that, we entertain them. I don't know whose job it is to do what you're talking about. Could be government, but then you can't have them watching themselves. Maybe it's the people's job to tell someone that they want to know this stuff. But who speaks for the people? And who do they tell? Maybe nobody's got that job?"

Paul jumps in. "I gotta say that was a fascinating story. But a normal person is busy with work and family and trying to get in a bit of golf. How's a normal person to get involved in being a change maker, either as a volunteer official of some sort or as just a person who writes letters and calls their officials? There's no time. And even if there were time, how could any normal person understand all the acronyms and laws and regulations and procedures. You can't possibly know who's on first. So to speak up about anything would be pretty stupid."

He continues. "I'm glad you all told the feds to clean up that mess. It's nice to know some local officials have the guts and knowledge to do that. I'm glad the stars aligned so that the Coconut Road tainted earmark got caught in the presidential campaign season and everyone everywhere could show they were tough on crime and waste by supporting the correction. I'm glad you won. But I sure don't know how I or my friends could ever help do something like that. We'd be doing good just to follow the story in the news. And then, I bet, we wouldn't keep all the details straight."

"You can't blame people for being angry," says Richard. "The schools don't teach kids how they can follow or get involved in government policy-making. The media forget that they're not just private corporations that exist to expand their markets and profits. They're the only private corporations specifically named in the U.S. Constitution and protected to give citizens the information needed to keep a democracy a democracy. Even though they get the spectrum space from the public, they think they owe nothing to the public—it's just the way the culture has developed. We're lucky people that some people are smart enough to know when something is wrong. It's just too bad that no one has a clue about how to fix things. All most of us can do is vote. And then how's a person to know if they are getting the right information or not. That's why people either don't vote or vote for a familiar name or vote a straight party line. Too bad! Parties may have good candidates, and sometimes they have scoundrels."

"I agree that it's hard for the public to keep it all straight," I say. Why even on single stories, like the Coconut Road coverage, it's possible for the media itself to get it wrong. One of the major national TV networks called the Board of County Commissioners to get a statement on why the MPO turned down Coconut Road. CNN didn't know that the Board of Commissioners is a different governing body from the Metropolitan Planning Organization. The secretary who answered passed the phone to the then Chair of the Board of Commissioners. Ray took the call. He got himself on national TV talking about how wonderful he was to support returning this tainted earmark to the feds. The truth, if you look at the record, is that he was one of the few on the MPO who voted against returning the money and one who had worked hard to block the MPO efforts. Who cares if he lied? He said what was good for him politically. This kind of error and self-serving activity happens all the time. Sometimes it's intentional. Sometimes it happens when people are too lazy or too incompetent to find the truth. Probably happens everywhere, not just in politics."

Richard take his turn. "We do ourselves a great disservice by not enabling everyone to know how to have a say in correcting what's wrong. But I don't know how you get the information out in a clear and simple and accurate way. I just hope we don't ignore the people in this democracy to the point where we are no longer a democracy and where people feel compelled to start a revolution in the streets. That would be a horrible legacy for our kids. And it would almost surely lead to power grabs and struggles that will be far worse than anything at present. At least we are still a system of laws and checks-and-balances and traditions. People have high expectations. We just need to make it easier for people to figure out how things work. And we need decent people to get involved and not shy away."

"That's for sure," Paul interjects. "All the good folks I know stay away from politics. So, how can you clean up and run a democracy if everyone wants to stay away?"

Richard says, "I just read this wonderful idea. Newton Minnow, who was FCC Chair fifty years ago, suggested that we might use some of the public's electromagnetic spectrum that used to be dominated by the broadcast channels before cable and satellite technologies. [1] Some spectrum could be auctioned off as space for a channel operated by entities that would educate the public on self-governing. Somehow there must be a way to do this that is generic and/or gives opportunity for all view points. Maybe it could be part of Public Broadcasting? In addition, such a channel could be used to do what most other democracies across the globe already do–permit all candidates who qualify for office to have a set amount of time to talk to the public. It's so absurd, not to mention the source of most of our political corruption, to have candidates in America need to raise extraordinary sums of money and make questionable promises to donors in return for being able to put a 30-second spot with little content on the air. Maybe we could learn how all those other countries in Europe manage a system like that?"

Richard is excited. "If all those young people can cause the corporate and economic powers of Egypt to pay attention with their "Google" and "Twitter" and "Face Book" messages, why couldn't we use these new media here? It's different though, we simply want people to know where and when they can have a say. Our system gives people that right; they just don't know how to use it. People' a in democracy would

221

know that their voice still mattered. Then they wouldn't get so angry. Could you even find ways for people to care about a civic affairs channel and to pay for it? There must be enough people who care about the future of American democracy. They'd have a self-interest in continuing what's good about our system. To create such a public channel, have significant public involvement and interest, provide free communication opportunities for candidates would go a long way to counter the Supreme Court decision to allow corporations to have the same value as a humans when it comes to financing campaigns. We could make this kind of change for America in the 21st century if enough people wanted it to happen."

Ted raises the visor on his hat, "I'll have to think about how that would work for our company. We'd need to find ways to still make the money we get for political ads, or find ways to cut costs enough so it didn't matter."

John has been sitting quietly. He says, "You all are getting too excited about this. Sure, Coconut Road is an interesting story. But on the grand scale, in the big picture, it's just one minor inconvenience to the people who had development plans east of I-75. They'll find another way to get what they want. Congressman Young's invisible empire is a constantly moving phenomenon. This is a little item. Yes, when the public—who doesn't know why we make the decisions we make—decides to interfere, it is irritating. But we weather those storms. I've yet to see strong enough sustained public understanding and interest in policy decisions to alter the plans that those of us who are businessmen make. Why would that change now? Corporations are the ones with the power and the money to keep America strong."

"Hey, John," interjects Paul. "All this stuff going back to the Statue of Liberty and all our history is about people—not big powers. You gonna throw all that out? If you do you lose a lot of what you need—customers, investors, honest employees, good will."

John is focused on Richard's idea for using spectrum for new civic education opportunities. He continues, "Richard, don't go dreaming about educating the public on making democracy work. Next thing you know, you'll also want this hypothetical television channel to offer courses on media literacy. It's O.K. that the public doesn't understand what public relations firms do for us, developing the content for our advertisements. Business needs ads to get the consumer focused on the simple reason why they should buy a product or a candidate and to repeat that ad often enough so the public remembers and goes out and supports what we want supported. We pay the PR firms big bucks for those services because they get us the results that bring profits from product sales and that win elections for our candidates Why would you want to mess with that? It might make a jittery economy even more jittery."

"Interesting ideas, Richard," I say. "You know, if you took your idea about auctioning free spectrum for the kind of channel you describe, you could follow Polsby's theory about how innovation happens. [2] You'd need to use all those social media digital electronics gadgets to do the 'policy incubation,' that is to generate a very widespread interest in the importance of this idea from stakeholders of all interests and convictions. That could easily take a couple years. Then, the timing would need to be right for codifying the law that turns this idea into policy. That would probably happen as a result of some crisis where it became clear that it's a common interest for us all to take the well-being of the American population seriously and to take seriously the people's role in America's democratic governing. At that point all stakeholder camps in political, corporate, and non-profit sectors will be at least willing to work out how to implement this idea. The idea can then become reality through the skillful informal negotiating of 'policy entrepreneurs' who are respected enough to be part of the many conversations needed to find the language of a law to use spectrum this way and to establish what is deemed a fair system of governance over such a new channel. And, don't forget you need your design to make this channel attractive enough that the public and the candidates will actually care and want to use it. That's change making!

"You know," I continue, "for as long as there have been written records of how humans behave, stories of change makers like the four I've told you continue to happen. People who are skeptics continue to argue. People view things differently. The struggles come between those who benefit from the status-quo and those who want more."

"Power is very seductive," I note, "as is wealth and prestige. Those fortunate enough to hold positions that confer power, wealth and prestige tend not to want to share what they have. I think it amazing that civilization has moved as far as it has toward recognition of democratic self-governance, toward human rights."

"I am concerned," I added, "that the global financial collapse of 2008 was triggered by a level of greed and arrogance beyond any before—largely because of the new technologies. The rationalization of those within the system who might have prevented some of the problems was triggered by personal levels of self-protection and fear beyond any before—greater because of the vastness of the consequences to innocent people. It has always been a given in western civilization that those with much should remember those with less. It's evident throughout history and literature. It's been a given in all the major religions that there is a human responsibility to care for one's neighbors. It's been an underlying premise behind the popularity of democracy as a form of governing that government 'of, for, and by the people' is the most stable, most fair and strongest way to manage civic affairs and stability over time."

Paul tilts his cap and joins in. "Whether we can keep the principle of concern for the larger civilization going for another generation, another century is a serious question. Will enough individuals think seriously about critical issues, contemplate the consequences, and evaluate their options? I get my kicks out of just playing. Fine with me to hear news in "Tweets" and soundbites. Somebody's got to figure out how to use these new toys to assist real problem solving."

He continues. "I don't see many role models that can prove to me that there's benefit for an ordinary guy like me to take the initiative and show the courage and the persistence required to be a change maker. Tell me before I jump off a cliff what's in it for me? It probably just comes down to an individual's own convictions about what matters. Maybe when it comes to taxes people will care. To get them to understand that it benefits everyone when there's work, education, good health, clean water and air and safety may be more complicated. The over-taxed thing sure pisses me off. I'd be happy to see things on that end change."

Ted says, "Maybe if the media saw some way that an idea like this could be profitable, there'd be support for it–if our companies thought that you could make money telling people about civic affairs. But Richard's idea will only work if it fits someone's self interest. And interest has to last so it's not just a flash in a pan. The public says it cares about its kids and grandkids futures, but that caring usually gets lost in the chaos of fixing the flat tire, paying the bills, taking kids to 'Chucky Cheese' for lunch, and collapsing in exhaustion to watch a movie. Don't know how you get long-range thinking in 21st century style—maybe the electronic toys can help. Using them in connection with a new channel. I'll think about it."

I stood up.

The train pulled into my station.

"It's time for me to leave. I appreciate your listening to these four stories and giving me your reactions. I hope you'll each take to heart all these nickel-and-dime efforts from people who care enough to try to change the world for the better–for themselves, for those around them and for the next generation. Nickel-and-dime change seems small against the backdrop of major global problems, but most people can only be spectators to global, even national, policy abuse. More important, it takes a paradigm change at ground level before one can bring change at the national and global level. Don't forget that there is an interdependence between holding national office and the local people they tend to ignore. I hope you might use these stories to prompt future efforts to make change. And I hope you will have stories of your own to tell others about the satisfaction of being change makers. It is individuals whose nickel and dime efforts bring the change and the hope for tomorrow that we continue to seek."

Epilogue

This is a memoir of my experience working with ordinary people who found themselves at a life-changing moment when they stopped to say "How dare they..." Their anger and ethics drove them to engage with dragons. They became change-makers. Their random small actions changed lives. Each tree they planted helped create a forest. Each nickel and dime of change contributed to make a dollar. They become extraordinary people. They brought a dance, an inspiration. They became participants in life, not spectators. Consider the thoughts of those who are known to us all as change makers:

THINKING PEOPLE THINKING:

"Action is the stream; contemplation the spring. They're two aspects of the same thing."
THOMAS MERTON

"I am the master of my fate; I am the captain of my soul."
NELSON MANDELA kept William Ernest Henly's poem "Invictus" in his Robben Island cell all those years of hard labor.

"The antithesis between the world and the church must be borne out in the world. That was the purpose of the incarnation."
DIETRICH BONHOEFFER, Pastor killed in Nazi Concentration Camp shifted his thinking from traditional sharp distinction between politics and religion because he saw the corrupt political authority in Germany and thought for the church to ignore or serve that regime perpetrated monstrous results.

"For an idea that does not first seem insane, there is no hope."
ALBERT EINSTEIN, the Nobel Prize winner who also stated that imagination matters more than knowledge.

DARING TO BE A CHANGE MAKER
"To dare is to lose one's footing momentarily, not to dare is to lose oneself.
SOREN KIERKEGAARD

"One man with courage makes a majority."
ANDREW JACKSON, military leader in newly forming United States and U.S. President

"Go, go, go," said the bird. "Humankind cannot bear very much reality."
T.S. ELIOT

AT THE END OF THE DAY
"Knowledge will forever govern ignorance, and a people who mean to be their own governors, must arm themselves with the power knowledge gives. A popular government without popular information or the means of acquiring it, is but a prologue to a farce or a tragedy or perhaps both."
JAMES MADSION, U.S. President

"The final enigma of history is therefore not how the righteous will gain victory over the unrighteous, but how the evil in every good and the unrighteousness of the righteous is to become overcome.
REINHOLD NIEBUHR, 20th century commentator on politics and culture, theologian

"Man does not live by GNP alone."
PAUL SAMUELSON, Economist

"Eyes cannot focus unless the imagination can see."
MARK TWAIN, (Samuel Clemens)

Two final comments.

I had a good friend named Newell Mack, a Harvard graduate, who never ceased to be irritated by the university's insistence that he should identify himself by title and by institution of employment. He maintained that it would be far better for all institutions to list people by their accomplishments than their titles.

I once gave a speech to honor Dr. Josephine Murray, founder of the Bunting Peace Fellowships at Radcliffe. I drew my speech from a book I'd read at The College of Wooster, *The Dancing Bees* by Karl Von Frisch. The book spoke of the deviant bees in a colony. Their daily work is not focused on contributing honey to the hive as do most of the workers. They are the heartbeat of the colony because their job is to venture off to find new sources of pollen, to identify where the colony can go when the current supply of pollen is used. They are the change makers, as were the Radcliffe fellows whose work linked research to real world application.

May what matters in life be your accomplishments that contribute to those around you, not your titles. May the rigors of living as a change maker bring a sparkle to your eye, love to your heart and the joy to the hearts of those around you.

End Notes

Counterpoint One:

1 Ladd, Everett Carl, "Public Opinion: Questions at the Quinquennial," *Public Opinion*, April/May, 1983.

2 Johnston, Carla Brooks, *Raising Myself,* Cambridge, MA: Parlance, 2010. Available on amazon.com

The First Story:

1 Wood, John B., "We came to save city from crooks," <u>Boston Globe</u>, Boston, February 19, 1971.

2 Juda, Daniel P., "Mayor Fires City Auditor in Somerville," <u>Boston Globe</u>, February 19, 1971. p.1.

3 Wood, Ibid. 2/19/71.

4 Author interview with Jim Bretta, Executive Director of Community Development, City of Somerville, December 3, 1996, Kelly's Diner, Somerville.

5 "Spotlight," <u>Boston Globe</u>, February 11, 1971, p.1f.

6 Johnston, Carla B., <u>Under the Interstate,</u> Boston: National Endowment for the Arts City Options Grant and the Massachusetts Department of Communuty Affairs, 1975., p. 46, 48, 63, 67, 150

7 Author interview with former Somerville resident, 10/96.

8 <u>Boston Globe</u> , February 11, 1971

9 Author interview with Robert W. Hilliard, December 3, 1996, Reading, MA.

10 Robert W. Hilliard interview.

11 Johnston, <u>Under the Interstate</u>, p i.

12 Author interview with Pat LaColla, December 2, 1996, Quincy, MA.

13 Author Interview with Maureen Amerol Hilliard, Vice-Principal, Lincoln Park Community School, Somerville, December 3, 1996, Reading, MA

14 Author interview with Pearl Morrison, Principal of West Somerville Neighborhood School, Somerville 12/12/96.

15 Morrison interview.

16 Morrison interview.

17 Author interview with Gloria Albano, Human Resources Director, MA Office for Medical Assistance, Boston, 12/10/97

18 Author interview with Fran Caruso, Lincoln St., Somerville, 12/11/96.

19 Caruso interview.

20 Caruso interview.

21 LaColla interview.

22 LaColla interview.

23 LaColla interview

24 LaColla interview

25 Author telephone interview with Barbara Harkins, Hyannis, MA 12/19/96

26 Harkins interview.

27 <u>Somerville Journal</u>, March 1967

28 LaColla interview

29 Bretta interview.

30 Author interview with State Rep. Patricia Jehlan, 11/26/96.

31 "Letters to the Editor," <u>Somerville Journal,</u> 11/6/68

31 "Brennan, Board Lash 'Invaders' of Local Schools," <u>Boston Record American</u> 11/19/68

32 <u>Boston Herald Traveller</u> ,3/2/69.

33 LaColla interview.

34 Bretta interview.

35 Maureen Hilliard interview.

36 Jehlan interview.

37 <u>Somerville Journal,</u> August 21, 1968

38 Harkins interview.

39 Harkins interview.

40 <u>Boston Record American</u>, 7/19/69 and U.S. Government Printing Office, "Hearings Before the Select Committee on Nutrition and Human Needs of the U.S. Senate, Part II," Washington, D.C., July 9. 10, 11, 1969

41 Jehlan interview.

42 "Letters to the Editor," <u>Somerville Journal</u>, 1/23/69.

43 LaColla interview.

44 Basingstoke, Nicholas, "The People's Choice," <u>Boston Sunday Globe Magazine</u>, December 7, 1969

45 Basingstoke, <u>Ibid</u>.

46 Basingstoke, <u>Ibid</u>,.

47 Robert W. Hilliard interview

48 Basingstoke, Ibid

49 Basingstoke, Ibid

50 Robert W. Hilliard interview.

51 LaColla interview.

52 Maureen Hilliard interview.

53 Bretta interview.

54 <u>Record American</u> 10/16/69 p 57.

55 Basingstoke, <u>Ibid</u>

56 Basingstoke, <u>Ibid</u>

57 Basingstoke, <u>Ibid</u>

58 <u>Record American</u> 12/11/69

59 Bretta interview.

60 Maureen Hilliard interview.

61 Maureen Hilliard interview.

62 Robert W. Hilliard interview.

63 LaColla interview.

64 Bretta interview.

The Second Story:

1 The Business School at Harvard and at Columbia prepared a case study for use in their classes to focus on how to facilitate both Executive and Legislative branches of an organization working toward common objectives.

2 *1977 MBTA Itemized Budget and Report of the Advisory Board Budget Committee and a Complete Reference on the MBTA,* (Approved by the Full 79 Member Advisory Board of Mayors and Selectman 12/30/76) Carla B. Johnston, Chief Budget Analyst for MBTA Advisory Board of Mayors and Selectmen, Robert Kiley, Chairman of MBTA responsible for Original Budget Submission

3 MBTA Advisory Board Budget Office, *Public Transportation Financing: A Survey of Options,* October, 1976. Carla B. Johnston, Chief Budget Analyst.

The Third Story:

1 *Effects of Nuclear War*, Washington, D.C., U.S. Office of Technology Assessment, 1979, p. 27 and p. 112

2 Lewis, Kevin, "The Prompt and Delayed Effects of nuclear War," *Scientific American*, New York, July, 1979. www.scientificamerican.com

3 All location quotes were submitted to "The Front Line: Civilian Defense from Nuclear Weapons," New Century Policies Educational Programs, Boston, MA 1981f.

4 Lawrence Wittner, "The Nuclear Freeze and Its Impact," *Arms Control Today,* Washington, D.C.: The Arms Control Association, December 2010. (A good synopsis of the Freeze movement and the context.

5 Katz, Arthur M., *Life After Nuclear War,* New York: Ballinger Publishing Company, 1982, Chapter 6. This provides data on post attack difficulties with food supply.

6 See Johnston, Carla, *Reversing theNuclear Arms Race,* Cambridge: Shenkman Books 1986, Forward by Rear Admiral Gene R. La Rocque, U.S. Navy (Ret.) p. 71f gives further explanation of FEMA

Leaning, Jennifer, Leighton, Matthew, Lamperte, John, Abrams, Herbert L. *Programs for Surviving Nuclear War: A Critique*, Chicago, *The Bulletin of Atomic Scientists*, June 1983

The Fourth Story:

1 The term 'earmark' generally means any expenditure for a specific purpose that is tucked into a larger piece of legislation going through Congress (like an authorization or appropriations bill.) Earmarks are

usually inserted into a bill at her request of a member of Congress for a project in their district or state—part of the long practiced 'bring home the bacon' aspectm of Congressional politics.

2 Carla Brooks Johnston, "Hijacking the U.S. Constitution: The Inside Story of Coconut Road," unpublished article, April 27, 2008.

3 Congressman Don Young, Chair of the U.S. House of Representatives Committee on Transportation and Infrastructure, Letter for Lee County MPO Chair, John Albion, January 23, 2006. Also Congressman Connie Mack, 14th District of Florida, Letter to Lee County MPO Chair, John Albion, January 31, 2006,

4 The language within the earmark was changed during a process called "bill enrollment," when technical corrections are made to legislation before being sent to the president. Such corrections include changes to punctuation, section numbers or updates to reflect final actions taken by the House and Senate.

5 "Highway Technical Corrections Act of 2007—Senate, April 16, 2008. See Senator Nelson (D-FL) comments Page:S3049.

6 Ryan Hiraki, "I-75 May Get $10 Million in Detour; Coconut Interchange Cash Could Be Used," *The News Press*, Fr. Myers, FL, August 9, 2007.

7 Julio Ochoa, "Report shows someone edited federal transportation bill," *Naples Daily News,* Naples, FL, Published on line August 8, 2007 and updated August 9, 2007.

8 Paul Kane, "A Congressman's $10 Million Gift for Road is Rebuffed," *Washington Post,* August 17, 2007.

9 "Washington Post On-Line Capitol Briefing: Paul Kane Reports on Congress. Posted at 4:45 PM ET, 08/17/2007

10 Greg Gordon and Erika Bolstad, "Federal investigation targets Alaska's congressman," *McClatchy Newspapers,* August 17, 2007 11:03:50 PM

11 Congressman Connie Mack, Member of House Transportation and Infrastructure Committee and representative for 14th Florida Congressional District, Letter to MPO Chair Johnston, August 21, 2007.

12 Laura McGann, "Coconut Road, The Other Side," TPM Muckraker. con, August 24, 2007. 1:51 PM.

13 Jack Schenendorf, Of Counsel, Covington and Burling LLP, "Statement on I-75/Coconut Road Interchange Project. Previously, he served as staff for House Committee on Transportation and Infrastructure for nearly 25 years and between 1995 and 2001, was their Chief of Staff working with Congressman Young.

14 *The New York Times* Editorial Board, "A Congressional mystery: Quid Pro Coconut," *The New York Times,* New York, January 8, 2008, posted electronically 5:20 PM.

15 George Will, "The Earmark Culture Thrives in Washington," February 7, 2008. George F. Will, a 1976 Pulitzer Prize winner whose columns are syndicated in more than 400 magazines and newspapers worldwide.

16 Susan Crabtree and Manu Raju, "Reid wants DOJ probe of Coconut Rd." *The Hill,* 4/15/08, posted 7:01PM ET

17 *New York Times Editorial,* "The Road to Somewhere Shady," *The New York Times,* April 21, 2008

18 Paul Kane, "Senate Seeks Inquiry Into Earmark Change," *Washington Post,* April 18, 2008, p. A09

19 Susan Crabtree, "Senate Calls for Probe of Coconut Rd.," *The Hill, Posted 4/17/08 7:46 PM {ET}*

20 Edward Epstein and Colby Itkowitz, "House Speaker Wants Ethics Probe of Highway Bill Earmark Change," *CQ Today Online News, 4/17/08,1:27 PM and 2:49 PM*
Adam Snider, "SAFETEA-LU Corrections Bill Heads to Bush With Enough Votes to Override Possible Veto," June 3, 2008

21 Greg Gordon and Erika Bolstad, "Federal investirgation targets Alaska congressman," *McClatchy Newspapers,* August 17, 2007, 11:03 PM

22 "Highway Technical Corrections Act of 2007—Senate, April 16, 2008." *Congressional Record.* See Senator Nelson (D-FL) comments Page: S3049.

Counterpoint Five and Conclusion:

1 Newton N. Minnow, "A Vaster Wasteland," *The Atlantic,* April, 2011.

2 Nelson W. Polsby, *Political Innovation in America,* New Haven, Yale University Press, 1984.

Author Biography

Carla Lee Brooks Johnston earned a B.A. in Religion from the College of Wooster in Ohio, and an M.A. from Andover Newton Theological School in Boston. She was later awarded three post-graduate fellowships at Harvard. She married, raised two children, provided a home for two foster children and a number of international exchange students. Her career has combined being a university professor, author of nine books, and a public policy maker (both as administrative head of government agencies and as two term Mayor of Sanibel Florida.) Her focus is strategic planning, effective budgeting and the role of the media in public policy. She has lectured in 34 countries on 6 continents.

She thrives on encouraging people to become change makers who take initiative, use courage and persistence to improve their own lives and that of those around them. She delights in opportunities that enable the growth of insight, wisdom and sensitivity needed to spread hope especially in situations where despair seems the norm. She considers herself most fortunate to have been able to help stimulate a new era for Somerville, MA, a city that faced huge problems in the 1960s-1970s; to work with a new team of leaders to curb the run-away budget of the metropolitan Boston transportation authority in the 1970s; to head the Boston metropolitan planning agency introducing programs to link planning to actual development in areas where local jurisdictions crossed and useful progress could only be realized by integrating previously separate funding (transportation, environmental protection, housing, etc.); in the 2000s, as an elected official, she was pleased to bring closer collaboration between biologists and engineers in setting water release policies that damage SW Florida; and as chair of the Metropolitan Planning Organization, she was pleased that it was possible to return a corrupted $10M federal earmark for a road not wanted to the U.S. Congress and to stimulate work that furthered the efforts to end earmark corruption. She calls her work "doing three dimensional crossword puzzles."

www.carlabrooksjohnston.com

241

www.ingramcontent.com/pod-product-compliance
Lightning Source LLC
Chambersburg PA
CBHW031152270326
41931CB00006B/236